NATIONAL

bus company

the early years

Kevin Lane

Contents

Front cover: Newly repainted in NBC poppy red, Red & White L1060 (10 AAX), a 1960 Bristol Lodekka FL6G, climbs through Caerphilly *en route* for Newport in November 1972. *John Jones*

Back cover (upper): Pool Valley, Brighton, plays host to Southdown Leyland Leopard PSU3/Weymann 155 (EUF 155D) loading for East Grinstead in April 1976. *Charles Dean / Author's collection*

Back cover (lower): Western Welsh U167 (JBO 162E), a Plaxton-bodied AEC Reliance, a long way from home on tour duties at Keswick in September 1975. *Charles Dean / Author's collection*

Title page: Alder Valley Leyland National 108 (KCG 608L) prepares to leave Oxford for home in October 1973. *John Jones*

The Publisher would like to thank National Express for permission to reproduce the National typeface and logo.

First published 2004

ISBN 0 7110 3023 5

Published by Ian Allan Publishing an imprint of Ian Allan Publishing Ltd, Hersham, Surrey KT12 4RG.

Printed in England by Ian Allan Printing Ltd, Hersham, Surrey KT12 4RG.

Code: 0411/B1

Introduction

FOR someone whose interest in buses blossomed during the National Bus Company era it is sometimes easy to forget that it is nearly 20 years since its dismemberment (and that I was still at school at its inception!). The corporate image, at its height by the mid-1970s, was all-encompassing; the double-arrow symbol could be encountered all over England and Wales. Buses were either red or green, while coaches were white —so different from today's multi-coloured industry. In this book I have attempted to illustrate the story of NBC's first seven years or so, until c1975/6, before the implementation of Market Analysis Project (MAP). The results from the various MAP surveys brought local involvement, via the county councils, back to bus services. This more localised thinking later saw the reversal of the prevailing 'big is best' policies, with the break-up of many of the larger companies and to their eventual privatisation. It is therefore a convenient time to end this review.

The period covered here was one of great change, as operations were consolidated and rationalised. There were many casualties, of course, and many familiar names were consigned to history (although some were to return, albeit in a different guise, during the 1980s). It was with some sadness, therefore, that we lost such operators as Brighton, Hove & District, Hebble, Midland General, North Western, Standerwick, Stratford Blue and Wilts & Dorset, to name but a few. There were new operators formed as well; many long-established coach operators were absorbed by the formation of the new National Travel units, whilst the fictitiously named Alder Valley was created in 1972 by the merger of Aldershot & District and Thames Valley. Other new creations included London Country Bus Services, while former independent operators also joined the fold to create new subsidiaries, such as Provincial and Venture. It should perhaps be remembered that there was much unpheaval generally within the bus industry at this time. Many municipal operators in the conurbations disappeared, swallowed up by the Passenger Transport Executives or merged to form larger units, while many of those that did survive found themselves with new names and new images following the 1974 local-government restructuring. (Who would have guessed that Thamesdown buses ran in Swindon?) At least London's buses were still red!

With regard to the vehicles themselves, the new regime had to get to grips with a varied (and, in many cases, elderly) collection of fleets. Although the early 1970s was dogged by lengthy delivery times for new vehicles and a lack of spares for the buses already in stock, by the middle of the decade the fleet was as standardised as it would be. Armies of Bristol RE, LH and VR types, along with Leyland Atlanteans, Nationals and Leopards, were everywhere (anyone feel nostalgic?) while most of the older stock was disappearing fast. Variety could still be found, however. Fords and Bedfords were bought as a stop-gap measure, and in localised areas such types as Routemasters and vehicles inherited from takeovers could be encountered, but these had to be sought out. Minibuses were beginning to make an appearance here and there in specialised roles, the first of what would turn out to be a flood during the 1980s.

There was also the thorny issue of liveries. Much has been written in the enthusiast press extolling the virtues of this or that livery. Certainly we lost some attractive and much-loved colour schemes, notably those of City of Oxford and East Kent, to name but two. However, the buses of the former Tilling group were largely red or green anyway, and some of the BET companies had been tidying their livery styles and simplifying fleetnames to give them a more modern appearance during the late 1960s. A new unifying image was to follow, and while the combination of poppy red or leaf green and National white looked smart when freshly applied, it tended to become shabby and faded if neglected. In some cases the new livery was applied without the benefit of white relief — definitely a low-point visually. This was, however, a distinctive era, and I hope that the following docs this period justice, particularly in terms of the balance between old and new liveries. Indeed, NBC's corporate image did miss a few corners right into the 1980s; London Country could muster two SM-class AEC Swifts which entered the new decade still in Lincoln green and yellow. Many of the colour pictures have come from the camera of a previously little-published photographer, the late Charles Dean, whose collection I now hold. Other photographers who have come to my aid are individually credited, but special thanks are due to John Aldridge for his hospitality and access, once again, to his collection. The usual thanks are due also to Maureen, my wife, but perhaps less so to my 17-year-old son, who wishes that I would write a 'proper' book sometime!

Kevin Lane
Dunstable
July 2004

City of Oxford's livery of red and duck-egg blue was sadly missed when replaced by NBC poppy red. New in 1971, Daimler Fleetline/Alexander 401 (TFC 401K) had just arrived in Oxford from Aylesbury when photographed in February 1973. *John Jones*

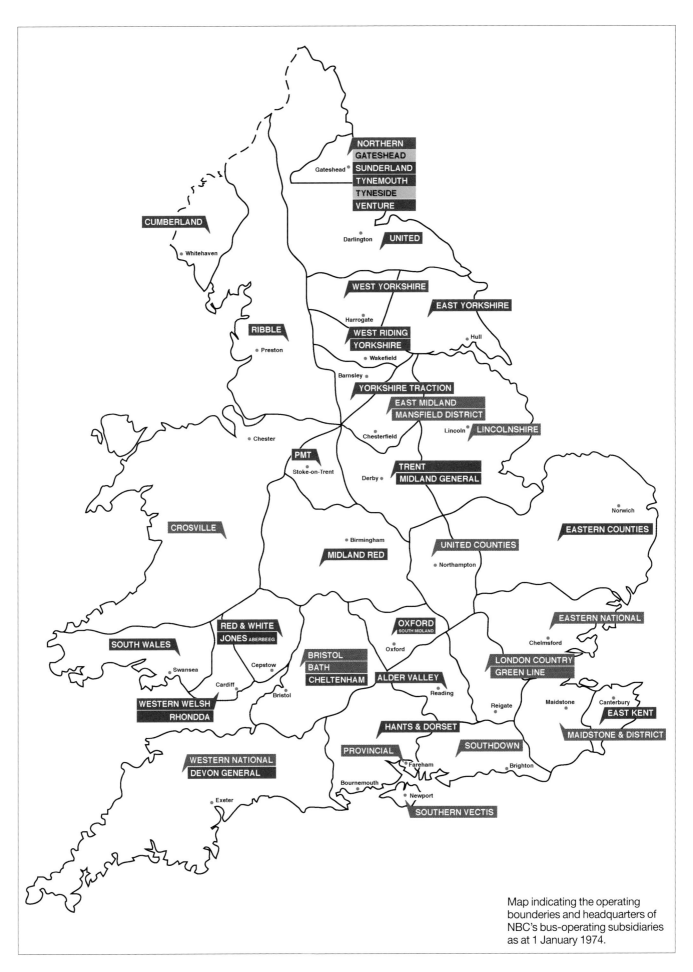

CUMBERLAND

NORTHERN
GATESHEAD
SUNDERLAND
TYNEMOUTH
TYNESIDE
VENTURE

Gateshead

UNITED
Darlington

Whitehaven

WEST YORKSHIRE

EAST YORKSHIRE

RIBBLE

Harrogate

WEST RIDING
YORKSHIRE

Hull

Preston

Wakefield

Barnsley

YORKSHIRE TRACTION

EAST MIDLAND
MANSFIELD DISTRICT

Chester

Chesterfield

Lincoln

LINCOLNSHIRE

PMT

Stoke-on-Trent

TRENT
MIDLAND GENERAL

Derby

Norwich

CROSVILLE

Birmingham

EASTERN COUNTIES

MIDLAND RED

UNITED COUNTIES

Northampton

EASTERN NATIONAL

RED & WHITE
JONES ABERBEEG

OXFORD
SOUTH MIDLAND

SOUTH WALES

Chelmsford

Oxford

LONDON COUNTRY
GREEN LINE

Cepstow

BRISTOL
BATH
CHELTENHAM

ALDER VALLEY

Swansea

Cardiff

Reading

Bristol

Reigate

Maidstone

Canterbury

EAST KENT

WESTERN WELSH
RHONDDA

HANTS & DORSET

MAIDSTONE & DISTRICT

SOUTHDOWN

PROVINCIAL

WESTERN NATIONAL
DEVON GENERAL

Fareham

Brighton

Bournemouth

Exeter

Newport

SOUTHERN VECTIS

Map indicating the operating
bounderies and headquarters of
NBC's bus-operating subsidiaries
as at 1 January 1974.

1969-1975 — an overview

THE formation of the National Bus Company, effective from 1 January 1969, did not happen overnight. Indeed, it could be argued to have been the culmination of a steady consolidation of bus operation over the previous 50 years. Without going too far back into the mists of time, a little history wouldn't be out of place here.

The major players in our story are the British Transport Commission (BTC), its successor from 1962, the Transport Holding Company (THC), and the British Electric Traction group (BET). Thomas Tilling was initially a London-based horse-bus operator; unable to extend his operations in the capital, he sought expansion elsewhere. BET, as its name implies, began as a tramway operator; in 1905 it set up a bus-operating subsidiary, which in 1912 became the British Automobile Traction Co Ltd. The two concerns steadily built up networks throughout the country and in 1928 set up the Tilling & British Automobile Traction Co Ltd (TBAT) — to co-ordinate operations and avoid wasteful competition. The situation inherited by the National Bus Company had more or less been created in 1942, when TBAT was disbanded and operators fell in with either Tilling or BET. Although most companies returned to that group with which they had formerly been associated, five were to change sides; Cumberland, Crosville and Lincolnshire passed to Tilling, while North Western Road Car and East Midland chose to join the BET group. Clement Attlee's Labour Government introduced the Transport Act 1947 which resulted in the setting-up of the BTC with the aim of the nationalisation, and thus integration, of inland transport. Tilling sold out to the state, but BET did not. Two other groups soon joined the BTC; in 1948 the transport activities of the Balfour Beatty group (itself mainly involved with the supply of electricity) were nationalised, to be followed by the Red & White group in 1950. Over the ensuing 20 years there would be further acquisitions (by BET as well as by the state sector) of individual companies, such as Neath & Cardiff (1950), Greenslades (1953) and West Riding (1967). Outside of the BTC and BET, bus operation in the United Kingdom was in the hands of London Transport (itself nationalised) and municipal and independent operators. The idea of a National Bus Company was announced in 1967, and, despite initial opposition, on 22 November of that year BET sold its bus interests to the THC.

The vehicle policies of the two groups were very distinctive and very different, as scrutiny of any 1950s/60s fleet list would soon reveal. The former Tilling fleets were highly standardised on Bristol chassis and Eastern Coach Works bodywork; both suppliers were also under the control of the BTC, and its operating companies were obliged to take their products (which were unavailable to almost everyone else). From time to time, however, vehicles — particularly coaches — were bought from other manufacturers, often to meet specialised requirements; Southern Vectis, with its penchant for Bedfords, perhaps springs to mind. The situation in the BET camp was more relaxed, with much more variety encountered, and most major chassis and bodybuilders represented. Furthermore, the development of Daimler and Leyland rear-engined double-deckers from the late 1950s allowed them to steal a 10-year march in this field on the BTC/THC. However, as the 1960s progressed, Leyland was to achieve dominance in bus manufacturing through merger and takeover. In 1965 a share exchange gave it a 25% stake in Bristol, thereby allowing non-BTC customers to be supplied with Bristol chassis (and specifically BET to buy the RE model).

In the early years of the National Bus Company the need to modernise saw unusual vehicle types appearing in various fleets, sweeping away previous traditions. This was influenced by a number of factors including industrial unrest, which resulted in the poor availability of new vehicles and spares to keep the old ones running. In other cases there was a desire to introduce one-man operation; Hants & Dorset's first one-man-operated rear-engined double-deckers were six Roe-bodied Daimler Fleetlines (rather than Bristol VRs, as might have been expected) diverted from Provincial (now under NBC control) in 1971 in exchange for a similar number of Bristol RELLs. No 1904 (VRU 127J) is seen at Bournemouth in 1972.
Alec Swain / Author's collection

A further distinction between the two groups was in the application of livery styles. In the main, vehicles of the BTC/THC companies were either red or green with cream relief; coaches were cream with either red or green relief. There were exceptions, of course; Brighton, Hove & District adopted red with cream window surrounds and roof, introduced in 1939 after a co-ordination agreement was reached with Brighton Corporation. Open-toppers with some operators were all-over cream, whilst Royal Blue coaches of Southern/Western National were, appropriately, blue and cream. Also blue and cream were the buses of Midland General. Another individual treatment was the retention of olive green and cream (which livery had been inherited with the takeover of Orange Bros in 1934) for United coaches operating services between London and the North East.

The BET group offered much more variety in terms of colour, while signwriting was applied with more of a flourish, witness the MacKenzie-style script fleetnames on Southdown coaches (and revived in a small way in the mid-1980s). Another example was Black & White Motorways (actually under the joint BTC/BET ownership of Bristol, Midland Red and City of Oxford), whose coaches had a style all of their own.

One other difference to note was BET's fondness for small subsidiary companies — not common within the BTC — which were useful for management training and were retained for as long as their operating costs remained lower than those of larger subsidiaries nearby. Northern General, for example, had five subsidiaries, while it was commonplace for the names of bought-out independents to be retained, at least for a while, as a goodwill gesture.

As a result of the Transport Act 1968, the National Bus Company began trading on the first day of January 1969. It

Once-conservative fleets were also enlivened by takeovers of independents. Non-standard vehicles might be withdrawn without being operated, but generally operators got their money's worth from acquired stock. United Leyland Leopard/Plaxton 2016 (PHN 216F), seen leaving Sunderland for Stockton in January 1975, had been ordered by Wilkinson, Sedgefield, but was delivered to United following takeover in 1967. At that time the United fleet was very much the model of a Tilling company, the last non-Bristol types having recently been withdrawn, although the Leopard was to become common in most NBC fleets as the 1970s progressed. *Charles Dean / Author's collection*

Set to become the standard NBC single-deck bus, the Leyland National made its first appearance in service in March 1972. Pictured at Workington on 2 July in BET red is 'chassis' 00115, which later that month would be delivered to Northern as its 5K (UUP 825K). The National in the background is demonstrator DAO 251K (No 00001). *Charles Dean / Author's collection*

should be noted that the 1968 Act also saw the introduction of the first Passenger Transport Authorities (PTAs), which through their respective Passenger Transport Executives (PTEs) sought to co-ordinate operation of local buses in Manchester, Merseyside, Tyneside and the West Midlands. This naturally had a profound effect on the relevant NBC operators. In some cases working agreements were introduced, and, in the case of Tyneside (later Tyne & Wear) PTE, Northern General vehicles were painted in the PTE's yellow livery. On the other hand, North Western Road Car lost much of its bus operations in 1972, when SELNEC took over in the Manchester area, and a decision was made to divide the rest between Crosville and Trent. Similarly, Midland Red lost its services within the West Midlands area — along with six garages and 413 vehicles — to that PTE in December 1973, although the company continued to operate.

Although there had been much preparatory activity behind the scenes, there was little initial change as far as the public were concerned. The same buses and crews turned up at the same times at the same stops, and it is doubtful whether many people outside the industry were aware of the upheaval. A few changes

were implemented from Day One, however. The United outpost at Carlisle was transferred to Ribble, the latter gaining some very un-BET Bristol MWs, while Brighton, Hove & District passed to ex-BET Southdown (although BH&D's livery of red and cream was initially retained). Other changes during 1969 included the takeover of County Motors, Lepton (which had been owned jointly by BET's Yorkshire Traction and independent West Riding), and Mexborough & Swinton by Yorkshire Traction, of Birch Bros by United Counties and the absorption of Southern National by Western National. In South Wales, Jones Omnibus Services of Aberbeeg sold out to NBC on 18 April, passing to Red & White control and being allowed to retain its blue livery. Other 'tidying up' included Maidstone & District's taking over East Kent's two routes in the Hastings area and Bristol Omnibus's gaining the Western National services at Trowbridge.

A more significant development came in July, when Leyland and NBC became equal partners in Bristol Commercial Vehicles and Eastern Coach Works, while plans were in hand for a new integral rear-engined single-deck bus, also a joint Leyland/NBC venture. To be built at a new plant already under construction at Lillyhall, near Workington, the Leyland National would be available to other UK (and, indeed, overseas) operators as well as NBC. Although a prototype appeared at the 1970 Commercial Motor Show, the first would not enter service until 1972.

Bus orders for 1970, announced in August 1969, were for 1,320 vehicles, more than half of Bristol manufacture. The familiar BET/THC pattern was perpetuated; East Kent took only AEC chassis, for example, while many of the old Tilling companies bought only Bristol. However, the RE was also appearing in ex-BET fleets, including North Western, Southdown and Western Welsh. In the early 1970s, before the Leyland National came onto the scene in large numbers, the Bristol VR was becoming the standard NBC double-decker, even in some ex-BET fleets, with the RE and LH as the standard saloons. Ironically, the Leyland Leopard, once a BET favourite, was to become the NBC choice for coach chassis once the Bristol RE was dropped. A further blurring of the lines was evident as, for example, ex-BET operators began buying Bristol/ECW products and painting them in their traditional liveries — the early VRs of Southdown, for instance.

Further consolidation took place in 1970 with a number of operators entering state ownership. Luton Corporation went to United Counties on 1 January, while formerly independent Gosport & Fareham ('Provincial') became a new subsidiary on the same day. Also in January 1970 Newbury & District was absorbed by Thames Valley after 20 years of control. Another takeover of a municipal operator was that of Exeter, which passed to Devon General control on 1 April. One month later Northern General acquired a new subsidiary, taking over Venture, of Consett. However, the biggest event of the year was the transfer to NBC on 1 January of London Transport's Country Area, which became London Country Bus Services. In terms of fleet size, London Country (1,303) was the fifth-biggest bus company in the UK, behind London Transport (6,591), SELNEC (2,428), West Midlands PTE (2,103) and Midland Red (1,738). In 1973 London Country would overtake Midland Red to become the biggest NBC subsidiary, after the latter lost services to WMPTE.

The rationalisation of the NBC subsidiaries carried on apace in 1971, particularly in South Wales, where BET had been dominant. United Welsh, Neath & Cardiff and Thomas Bros of Port Talbot all disappeared into South Wales, while Rhondda was absorbed by Western Welsh. Elsewhere in the west, Grey Cars merged with Greenslades, and Devon General came under Western National control but retained its identity. Stratford Blue was absorbed completely by Midland Red, having been owned by the latter since 1935, while ex-THC coach operator South Midland Motor Services was transferred from Thames Valley to ex-BET City of Oxford. The year also witnessed the development of a stronger management style at the top of NBC which was prepared to overrule individual company management.

Effectively a typical pre-NBC coaching line-up, recorded at Bourton-on-the-Water, Gloucestershire, in the summer of 1969. Two Hants & Dorset Bristol RELH / Duple Northern keep company with an earlier coach from the same fleet, Bristol MW6G/ECW 895 (AEL 3B), while alongside is another Bristol MW6G/ECW, Eastern National 383 (1 BXB). The Eastern Counties vehicle obscured by passengers is Bedford VAM/Duple CB837 (LNG 837E). *Colin Martin*

More long-established names were to disappear in 1972. Thames Valley and Aldershot & District merged to form the fictitiously-named Alder Valley, whilst neighbouring Hants & Dorset took over Wilts & Dorset, which had been under its control since 1964 and had shared the same legal address from 1969. In the Midlands consolidation was taking place, with Midland General absorbing Notts & Derby and itself coming under the control of Trent in January (although it would not be fully absorbed until 1976). Two months later Trent acquired the Buxton and Matlock depots of North Western Road Car following the latter's dismemberment. Similarly, Crosville gained that company's Northwich and Macclesfield garages (and 119 vehicles) and its portion of the garage at Biddulph, shared with PMT. Crosville also gained former Western Welsh (latterly South Wales) territory in West Wales. The old BTC/BET lines were definitely disappearing.

If we were to have a 'national' bus company, it followed that an image to reflect this should be developed. As noted above, a variety of livery styles and applications was inherited in 1969, and some sort of order would eventually have to be implemented. Although there had been a certain degree of simplification of old liveries and fleetnames in some areas, and coaches were taking on a common style (with a large fleetname on a broad coloured band, for instance), this was short-lived. It was the unified image of the Greyhound Corporation coaching network in the USA that inspired NBC's newly appointed chairman, Frederick Wood. (British Railways had gone through a similar re-branding in the 1960s, sweeping away much of the previous individuality and emerging as the everything-blue British Rail.)

The first sign of the new NBC image was the appearance, from March 1972, of coaches in an all-white livery with 'N A T I O N A L' applied in alternate red and blue letters, together with a double-N symbol. The identity of individual operators was deemed unimportant, and a tiny underlined fleetname was placed begrudgingly over the front wheel-arch, although its prominence was later increased. There followed a bus livery; after a brief period with a third colour, blue, it was dictated that only two variations were allowed, poppy red or leaf green with a white relief (Jones Omnibus alone being allowed to remain in blue). A uniform fleetname style with the double-N logo was incorporated. Another development was a dual-purpose or 'local coach' livery of red or green below the waistline and white above. In former BTC fleets, where the Tilling influence was still strong, buses usually remained the same colour, just in a different shade. There was, therefore, little outward difference to a member of the travelling public to an Eastern Counties vehicle in 1963 or 1973. It was in those fleets inherited from BET fleets elsewhere that the difference was most apparent. East Yorkshire

By the mid-1970s National white was the order of the day. Pictured at Gretna in September 1975 are two Northern vehicles — Bristol RELH/Plaxton 5044 (NCN 816L) and Leyland Leopard/Plaxton 5018 (DCN 8D) — together with Southdown Leopard/Plaxton 1823 (UUF 323J), all on tour work. *Charles Dean / Author's collection*

In 1973 some 91 Bristol VRs were transferred to NBC from the Scottish Bus Group in exchange for Bristol FLFs, following 15 transferred from Alexander (Midland) to Eastern National in a separate deal two years previously. Pictured in Edinburgh on 28 March 1973, Eastern Scottish AA988 (LAH 489E) still carries full NBC livery and fleetname, having obviously been pressed into service immediately after acquisition from Eastern Counties. *Charles Dean / Author's collection*

went from dark blue to NBC blue and then NBC red, while London Country lost its attractive green with yellow relief as applied to early Atlanteans and Fleetlines, for instance. Moreover, the 'all-over' application of the new scheme sat uneasily on many older designs of bodywork. The need for this uniform image was understandable, of course, if only for economic reasons, but in some areas vehicles began to appear scruffy, the poppy red seeming to be more prone to fading. Where neighbouring operators chose the same colour, it could be difficult for passengers to differentiate; a London Country Leyland National in Luton looks rather like one from United Counties!

The year 1972 also saw the entry into service of the Leyland National, the first of which took up its duties with Cumberland in March as its 350 (ERM 35K). Other early recipients within NBC were Northern General, London Country and Crosville. A highly standardised integral design, the National was available in two lengths (10.3m and 11.3m), with dual or single door, and was powered by the Leyland 510 engine. It soon became a familiar sight, and production rose to around 22 per week. However, in-service testing ahead of initial deliveries was not as thorough as it might have been, resulting in many early problems. These troubles were gradually resolved in service, and all bus-operating NBC subsidiaries with the exception of City of Oxford eventually took delivery of the type. In some instances, operators were reluctant to take the National, but supply problems elsewhere in the bus industry — and Leyland's decision to cease production of the Bristol RE — meant that they had little choice for new buses.

Industrial relations in Britain were very poor during the early 1970s, the three-day week and the 1974 fuel crisis ensuring long delivery times for new vehicles and a poor availability of spares when they did arrive. Staff shortages and the many life-expired vehicles in need of replacement only compounded the problems. The NBC fleets of this period reflect this turmoil, with extensive hirings from other companies, stop-gap acquisitions of older vehicles and the reluctant purchase of non-standard types. Thus Fords and Bedfords appeared in fleets with no tradition of such types. Hants & Dorset and Alder Valley, for instance, each took 25 Ford R1014s with ECW bodywork (which at first glance resembled Bristol REs) along with smaller numbers of Plaxton-bodied examples. South Wales would ultimately receive a combined total of 83 Fords and Bedfords, whilst United Counties, formerly a typical THC operator, ran 69, mostly Bedfords. Even Southdown built up an impressive fleet of 40 Ford R1114/Duple coaches, the biggest within NBC.

As the 1970s progressed the all-over advertisement became a popular source of additional revenue, although the results were not always very tasteful. More restrained than some was Western Welsh Leyland Atlantean/Weymann LR3362 (364 ABO), promoting London & Manchester Assurance in Cardiff in April 1976. The apparent lack of a fleetname must have caused confusion amongst passengers. *Charles Dean / Author's collection*

From the late 1960s the Bristol/ECW combination, previously available only to state-owned operators, became commonplace in most ex-BET fleets; Southdown Bristol VR/ECW 538 (WUF 538K), still in the old green and cream but with NBC fleetnames, is seen at work in Brighton in April 1976. *Charles Dean / Author's collection*

As the decade wore on, more independent operators sold out to the state. In 1973 Hants & Dorset reluctantly gained King Alfred at Winchester, while Midland Red acquired Green Bus of Rugeley and Cooper of Oakengates and followed these with Harper Bros of Heath Hayes and Hoggins of Wrockwardine Wood in 1974 — some consolation for the work lost in the West Midlands. Also in 1974 Maidstone & District took on Streamline Coaches of Maidstone and Dengate of Rye. In the North East, United absorbed two County Durham independents — Gillett Bros of Quarrington Hill in October 1974 and Shaw Bros of Byers Green in January 1975. United Counties, already with Birch Bros (1969) and Luton Corporation (1970) under its belt, took over the services and eight coaches from the financially troubled Court Line Travel group in Luton in 1974 and the stage services only from York Bros, Northampton, in 1975. Four more acquisitions were incorporated into the newly created National Travel units (of which more anon): Don Everall Travel of Wolverhampton, taken over by NBC in 1973, was placed under the control of National Travel (Midlands) with effect from 1 January 1974, being joined in March by Worthington Motor Tours of Birmingham; also in March the Norwich division of Mascot Coaches was acquired jointly by Eastern Counties and National Travel (South East), which divided the spoils between them, while in August Wessex Coaches sold most of its operations and vehicles to National Travel (South West).

The same period saw further consolidation amongst the existing fleets: the Keighley-West Yorkshire operation was absorbed by the parent fleet in 1974, while Northern General was in the process of winding up its various subsidiary companies, a process completed by the beginning of 1976.

The biggest upheavals within NBC at this time concerned its coaching activities. At the beginning, the coaching operations of NBC became the responsibility of the Central Activities Group, which had control over those fleets — such as Black & White Motorways, Greenslades and Sheffield United Tours — that only ran coaches. To a certain extent operations carried on as before, although some reorganisation did take place. The Associated Motorways pool, for instance, carried on until 1974. This had been co-ordinating express services between the Midlands, London and South Wales and the South West for 40 years and had itself built up a unified image with regard to booking and publicity, but this did not extend to the vehicles of the individual operators involved. The need within NBC was to develop a unified image, and this was to come as a collection of National Travel companies was formed from 1973, to bring some order to what was hitherto a confusing situation.

It was inevitable that the early years of the new regime would see a review of operating territories and that this would result in casualties. Two companies to disappear were Midland General and North Western, the former to be finally absorbed by Trent, and the latter dismantled, its bus operations passing to Crosville, Trent and SELNEC. Seen in October 1969, before these upheavals, are Midland General Bristol LS6G/ECW 241 (XNU 422) and North Western AEC Reliance/Weymann 734 (LDB 734). The location is Matlock; although North Western operations here passed to Trent, neither vehicle illustrated would be around to witness it, both being withdrawn in 1970. The LS, however, would see further service within NBC, passing to Provincial at Fareham. *Tony Moyes*

Five National Travel units were set up and began operating early in 1974. National Travel (North East) was formed from Hebble and Sheffield United, National Travel (North West) brought together North Western and Standerwick, while National Travel (South East) comprised Tillings, Samuelsons and Timpsons, to which were later added the coaching activities of Eastern National and a half share in Mascot. National Travel (Midlands) at first had no vehicles of its own, instead hiring them in from various Midlands-based operators, but later acquired control of Everall and Worthington and in 1977 was merged with National Travel (North West) to form National Travel (West). The biggest of the new companies was National Travel (South West), encompassing Black & White, Greenslades, Shamrock & Rambler and Wessex. At first vehicles often carried the fleetnames of their constituents, but gradually the collective names would appear, although slipboards could be fitted to accommodate something different. Coaches were also hired from the predominantly bus-operating subsidiaries (which were not part of the National Travel organisation) when not required by their owners. However, as a unified route-numbering system was introduced from October 1973 and all coaches carried the same white livery, as far as the public was concerned they were all one and the same (except at busy periods, when independent coaches with 'on hire' stickers in the windscreen were pressed into service, and places such as Cheltenham coach station became altogether more colourful!).

By the mid-1970s NBC's image was more-or-less complete, and most of its vehicles carried corporate liveries. Standardisation was well on the way to completion. Vehicle orders for 1974 called for 488 Leyland Nationals and 344 Bristol VRs — just about half of the 1,650 new vehicles planned. The remainder comprised Leyland Atlanteans and Leopards, Bristol REs and LHs, a number of Ford and Bedfords and a few AEC Reliances. In contrast, the NBC orders for 1975 were for 1,140 vehicles — all Bristol or Leyland with the exception of five Scania/MCW Metropolitan and five Ailsa/ Alexander double-deckers, to be trialled by Maidstone & District. Neither type was to gain acceptance within NBC.

The idea of a monolithic operation, where 'bigger is better', was at its peak in the mid-1970s, making this a convenient time to end this review. As the decade progressed and passenger figures declined, local councils were taking more of an interest in transport and ways to support unremunerative services. This resulted in the Market Analysis Project (MAP) schemes undertaken between 1977 and 1982 to determine just what sort of service the passenger actually wanted in a given area. The results were far-reaching and, along with other factors, would ultimately decide the future of NBC.

In Yorkshire, Hebble Motor Services lost its stage services to become the coach operator of the West Riding group. It disappeared, along with Sheffield United Tours, to create National Travel (North East) in 1974. The old fleetnames lingered on the side of vehicles for a while, as apparent from this view of LJX 818H, a 1970 Leyland Leopard/ Plaxton, Newcastle-bound at Sheffield in March 1975. *Charles Dean / Author's collection*

The minibus did not feature too prominently in the NBC fleets of the early 1970s (and thank goodness for that, some may say!). Nevertheless, its use was on the increase, albeit in rural rather than urban areas. In a joint initiative commencing in November 1975 Eastern Counties and Norfolk County Council used this Deansgate-bodied Ford Transit, employing volunteer drivers and serving villages in the Holt and Fakenham areas. This photograph, at Brinton, was evidently a publicity shot taken before the service began; two months after delivery MB998 was found to have been given a registration (HEX 683N) that had already been issued, and it was duly re-registered as KCL 416N. *John Aldridge collection*

Alder Valley Services, or, to give it its proper (if more cumbersome) title of Thames Valley & Aldershot Omnibus Co Ltd, was the result of the merger on 1 January 1972 of former BET Aldershot & District Traction Co and ex-THC Thames Valley Traction Co, the combined operations being spread around Berkshire, Buckinghamshire, Hampshire and Surrey.

Aldershot & District Traction Co had always favoured locally produced Dennis chassis, and its double-deck intake between 1958 and 1965 can be summed up in two words — Dennis Loline. Its final double-deckers were the 50 Weymann-bodied examples bought in 1964/5. Seen c1970 working Guildford local route 30, 504 (AAA 504C) displays A&D's final livery style, with simplified fleetname replacing the traditional scroll used since 1923. *Author's collection*

One of the many AEC Reliances in the Aldershot & District fleet, Weymann-bodied 388 (388 AOU) passes through the north-Hampshire village of Greywell in August 1970 on the Odiham–Basingstoke route taken over in 1962 from independent Odiham Motor Services. The vehicle employed on this route was kept overnight at Odiham and maintained at Wilts & Dorset's Basingstoke garage. *Philip Wallis*

Although Aldershot & District was a long-standing customer for AEC and Dennis chassis, it took numerous examples of the Bristol RE once that model became available on the open market. One of the first batch of 15 new in 1970, 610 (UOU 610H), is seen in Reading in July 1971. *Alec Swain / Author's collection*

In vehicular terms the Thames Valley Traction Co was a typical THC operator, its bus fleet being almost entirely Bristol/ECW by the late 1960s, although that of coaching subsidiary South Midland included Bedfords. Not surprisingly Thames Valley was an early customer for Bristol's new, rear-engined VRT model, taking its first two in 1968, straight after its last FLF Lodekkas. Eleven more followed in 1969, including 502 (UBL 243G), seen when new at London Victoria about to return to Reading on service A; this ran via Ascot, whereas service B went via Slough and Maidenhead. *Author's collection*

In the late 1960s and early 1970s Thames Valley acquired a number of Bristol LS buses from fellow THC/NBC subsidiaries, including 155 (960 ARA), new in 1956 to Midland General and seen in 1971 loading in Reading for Bucklebury. *Alec Swain / Author's collection*

Prior to its rebuilding in the early 1970s, the bridge over the Thames at Marlow was subject to a 5-ton weight restriction. Buses could carry only 15 passengers across; presumably any others would have to walk! Thames Valley's requirement for small buses able to negotiate the bridge was met by a quartet of Bristol SUS4A/ECW saloons acquired from Bristol or Western National. Received from the latter source in 1969, 196 (668 COD) is seen crossing the bridge in June 1970 while *en route* for Maidenhead. *Philip Wallis*

The oldest Aldershot & District vehicles to enter the Alder Valley fleet were the survivors of a batch of 25 Strachans-bodied AEC Reliance coaches delivered in 1954. Still in A&D livery, 359 (MOR 601) was caught in Petersfield on a local route to Alton in June 1973.
Alec Swain / Author's collection

Aldershot & District had bought Dennis Lolines from 1958 until 1965, after which all deliveries had been single-deckers. Those Lolines dating from 1962 carried Alexander bodywork, such as 800 (458 EOT) at work in Guildford in August 1975.
Philip Wallis

Looking smart and fresh from repaint (note too the rear wheel discs) at Aldershot in March 1973 is Bristol RESL6G/ ECW 451 (YHO 635J), amongst the last buses delivered new to Aldershot & District before the merger with Thames Valley.
John Jones

Most of the double-deckers transferred from Thames Valley were Bristol Lodekkas of one sort or another. No 608 (WJB 225), an FLF6G dating from 1960, waits at traffic lights in heavy rain in High Wycombe in 1975. *Author*

The new company soon began to standardise on the Leyland National for its single-deck requirements. Large numbers were bought from 1973, although Bristol LH6Ls and Ford R1014s were also purchased during the period 1974-6. Leyland National 242 (LPF 600P) is seen at Victoria when almost new, in April 1976. This was one of a batch with dual-purpose seating and is on a service to Reading via Slough and Maidenhead, once the preserve of Bristol VRs and Lodekkas. *Charles Dean / Author's collection*

Alder Valley experienced vehicle shortages during the early years and as a result had to hire buses to cover. London Country Bus Services assisted between May and November 1973 with five RTs, the condition of which probably didn't endear them to the travelling public. Weymann-bodied 1950-vintage RT4102 (LUC 451), on loan from Windsor, heads out of Reading for Mortimer station in June. Service information was evidently not a priority! *Alec Swain / Author's collection*

At the time of the NBC takeover Bristol was still running a sizeable fleet of Bristol KSWs. By 1973 18 were left in the City fleet and four with Cheltenham District. As with many former BTC fleets it could also boast a few relegated to driver-training duties, as such often outlasting their passenger-carrying sisters. A pair of Bristol Omnibus KSWs, formerly 8192 (SHW 362) and 8148 (PHW 973), stand in the rain at Bath in May 1973. In the background is another training KSW and tree-lopper W120 (OHY 965), one of a number of highbridge KSWs that had come to grief over the years under St Luke's Road railway bridge at Bedminster. *John Aldridge*

The two Bristol KSWs that survived at Cheltenham beyond 1973 found themselves wearing NBC poppy-red livery, 'Cheltenham' fleetnames and an enlarged borough coat of arms; seen shortly before its demise, 8563 (WHW 821) of 1956 was one of the pair to be withdrawn early in 1973. The KSWs operating in Bristol soldiered on, four of them receiving repaints in NBC leaf green, and the very last — C8374 (WHW 815) — surviving until 29 May 1976, the last of its type in normal NBC service. *Colin Martin*

Not surprisingly, Bristol also ran many Lodekkas, including the prototype and first pre-production models. More mundane perhaps, is this 1965 FLF6B 7188 (CHT 531C), at work in Swindon in February 1973. Just 80p for the freedom of Bristol's services sounds a bargain, considering that the routes extended as far as Hereford, Oxford, Salisbury and Weston-super-Mare. Bristol's network in Wiltshire had been boosted by the acquisition in 1970 of the Western National outpost at Trowbridge, along with 24 buses comprising Bristol KSW, LS, FSF and FLF types. *John Jones*

Bristol REs entered the fleet from 1967, working alongside LS, MW and SU types. Pictured in Hereford bus station in August 1970 is 1098 (RHT 147G), a 1968 RELL6L/ECW.
John Jones

The 'Bristol Greyhound' fleetname applied to coaches from the early 1960s had its origins in Greyhound Motorways, acquired by Bristol in 1928. It survived on a variety of coaches until 1973, when Bristol's express routes were transferred to National Travel (South West). ECW-bodied Bristol RELH6G 2128 (974 WAE) arrives at London Victoria in April 1973, shortly before transfer.
John Aldridge

Although Bristol purchased the two prototype 80-seat VRs in 1970, it ran them for just three years. The company's first new VRs were a batch of eight 70-seat dual-door VRTs which began work on City services in April 1972. They received a double-deck version of the OMO livery, represented here by C5009 (EHU 368K), looking a little shabby, c1975. *Author's collection*

A former Tilling company, Crosville Motor Services had its headquarters in England, at Chester, but also served the whole of North and Mid-Wales. The oldest Crosville double-deckers to pass to NBC ownership were Bristol LDs, the company's last Bristol KSWs having been withdrawn by 1968. New in 1958 — towards the end of the LD's production run — DLB902 (884 CFM) is seen in Chester in June 1973, apparently fresh from a repaint into NBC colours, although the lack of any relief gives a rather drab appearance. DLB902 (**D**ouble-deck, **L**odekka, **B**ristol engine) would survive with Crosville until 1975. *Charles Dean / Author's collection*

It might be expected that a fleet such as Crosville would, by the early 1970s, be predominantly Bristol/ECW in its makeup. While this was largely true, there were nevertheless some decidedly non-THC vehicles; Bedford VAMs were chosen for a number of coaches, whilst Seddon RUs were bought in 1971/2. The latter year also saw the arrival of the first Leyland Nationals and the dismembering of North Western Road Car, whose operations had been substantially reduced by the loss of operations in Manchester to SELNEC. Crosville gained operations at Biddulph, Macclesfield and Northwich and, NWRCC having been a BET company, a mix of AEC, Leyland, Daimler, and Dennis vehicles, although Bristol REs were being delivered. Looking in fine fettle at Manchester Piccadilly while working from Macclesfield garage in July 1972, DAA505 (VDB 968) was one of 16 AEC Renowns new in 1963, the majority of which lasted with Crosville until 1979. *Charles Dean / Author's collection*

Crosville fell for the rather basic charms of the front-engined Bristol SC, taking 74 ECW-bodied SC4LKs between 1957 and 1961 for rural routes. New in 1960 and fitted with an all-plastic/fibreglass body, SSG664 (237 SFM) is pictured at the Sychnant Pass in June 1974, advertising the cinematic delights on offer at the Astra, Colwyn Bay. Crosville would rid itself of its last SC4LK by 1976. *Chris Lodington*

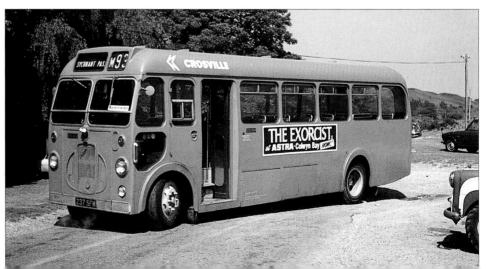

Following the acquisition of part of North Western came the transfer, from March 1972, of operations around Newcastle Emlyn and New Quay from Western Welsh; included were 11 Leyland Tiger Cubs, examples of which were also inherited from North Western. In April Crosville took over the former Western Welsh Lampeter outstation from South Wales Transport; SAA984 (WKG 283), seen loading in Aberystwyth in August 1973, was one of a pair of Willowbrook-bodied AEC Reliances thus acquired. *Chris Lodington*

Crosville raised a few eyebrows in 1971/2, when it took delivery of 100 Pennine-bodied Seddon RUs. Two early examples, EPG706/9 (KFM 706/9J), stand at Liverpool Pier Head when almost new in August 1971. *Chris Lodington*

The aforementioned Bedford VAM coaches were delivered in 1967 and 1969 and were bodied variously by Duple, Duple Northern and Plaxton, a total of 14 vehicles in all. In October 1973 CVT684 (NFM 684E), a 1967 VAM5 with Duple Northern bodywork, stands at the Square, Tregaron (about 20 miles southeast of Aberystwyth) beside the statue of the town's most famous son — Henry Richard (1812-88), MP for Merthyr Tydfil and the first Secretary of the League of Nations. *John Jones*

Cumberland Motor Services came under Tilling control from 1949, having been a BAT company since 1921. For several years after nationalisation Cumberland continued to receive Leyland vehicles, honouring previous agreements. From 1954, however, the first Bristols entered the fleet, preceded by a couple of Lodekka demonstrators in 1951 and 1953. A handful of Leyland PD2/12s survived into NBC days, but otherwise all double-deckers were Lodekkas of various types. No 511 (115 DRM), an FLF6G new in 1961, is seen on a works service in the mid-1970s — a reminder that Workington/ Whitehaven was still an area of heavy industry at this time.
Author's collection

Cumberland went through the familiar sequence for BTC/THC companies in buying Bristol LS, MW and RE saloons, as well as a few SCs. Representing the Bristol MW is 231 (AAO 34B), an ECW-bodied MW6G new in 1963 (albeit not entering service until the spring of 1964), one of 29 in the fleet. The vehicle is seen in September 1975, laying over at Keswick between journeys on a service to/from nearby Thornthwaite.
Charles Dean / Author's collection

The first Bristol REs and the last MWs were delivered in 1966, the REs continuing to enter the fleet until 1972. From the 1967 intake is 256 (KRM 262E), one of 12 Bristol RELL6Ls delivered that year, also seen at Keswick in September 1975.
Charles Dean / Author's collection

In 1969 Cumberland was operating coaches on a variety of chassis, consisting of Bedford VAL and VAM types and Bristol LS and MW models. The Bedford VAL, an uncommon type in either BET or THC fleets (although those operating with Southern Vectis and Hants & Dorset are well-known), found a niche in the North West, four entering the Cumberland fleet during the period 1965-7. Duple Northern-bodied 1303 (LAO 581E) is seen at Dumfries in June 1972, a month before withdrawal. *Geoff Mills*

For Cumberland, 1970 was the year of the Bristol LH, nothing else entering the fleet during that year and no other LHs being purchased before or since. Only one of the 18 was a coach, Plaxton-bodied LH6P 1310 (WAO 289H), used initially as team coach for Whitehaven Rugby League Football Club. This unique vehicle in the Cumberland fleet is pictured on a Lake District excursion at Keswick in July 1972. It subsequently gained National white livery and survived until 1978. *Charles Dean / Author's collection*

Coaches bought new in the 1972-4 period were all Duple-bodied Fords. The seven of 1972 were 45-seat R192s, numbered 801-7; 805 (ERM 805K) lays over at London's Battersea Coach Park in 1975. *Author's collection*

The East Kent Road Car Co was formed in 1916 by the amalgamation of five operators in the Canterbury/Thanet area. As a BET company, it purchased Leylands, Guys and Daimlers postwar. The Guy Arab double-decker remained in favour until 1957, and a number were still in stock in 1969. Posed in Canterbury garage yard during that year is GFN 927 (fleet numbers not being used until 1977), a Park Royal-bodied Guy Arab IV new in 1953. One of the last of its batch to be withdrawn, in 1973, it would then survive for a further two years in the service fleet. *V. C. Jones*

Successor to the Guy Arab was the AEC Regent V, also with Park Royal bodywork, bought between 1958 and 1967; indeed, it was the only double-deck type to be bought during this period, with the exception of a trio of AEC Bridgemasters new in 1962. Looking smart in NBC corporate colours, GJG 743D awaits custom at Canterbury in 1974. *Author's collection*

With production of the AEC Regent ceasing in 1969, East Kent had to look to other manufacturers for rear-engined double-deckers. Replacing Guy Arabs, 20 Park Royal-bodied Daimler Fleetlines were delivered in 1969, after which no more new double-deckers would be bought until 1976. RFN 969G looks good at work on Folkestone town service 106 on its first day in service, 27 July 1969. *M. D. C. Ansell*

The company bought the AEC Reliance for both bus and coach use for some 20 years; indeed, the last of the 1955 batch was withdrawn as the 1975 vehicles were entering service. The type accounted for all vehicles taken into stock in 1968, the year's deliveries comprising 25 Marshall-bodied buses and eight Willowbrook-bodied coaches. The first of the buses, OFN 708F, is seen at Canterbury early in 1969. *Lyndon Rowe / Author's collection*

Vehicles delivered in early NBC days carried traditional East Kent livery, as demonstrated here by Plaxton-bodied AEC Reliance WJG 138J outside Ashford garage when four months old in July 1971. *Alec Swain / Author's collection*

The white National livery looked fine on the more modern coaches but did not always sit too comfortably on older body styles, as its application disregarded mouldings and other features. East Kent DJG 612C, a Park Royal-bodied AEC Reliance of 1965, leaves Victoria Coach Station for Ramsgate in the summer of 1975. *John Aldridge*

East Midland Motor Services had been under BET control since 1930, and rolling stock inherited by NBC was mainly of Leyland and AEC manufacture. D43 (143 ENN) was an early (1960) Leyland Atlantean with lowbridge Weymann body, seen leaving Derby for Chesterfield in the summer of 1976.
Charles Dean / Author's collection

Although East Midland's buses became leaf green under NBC, prior to this they had carried an attractive livery of red and cream (and mustard, brown and cream before that). This is demonstrated by O510 (OAL 510F), a 1968 AEC Swift/ Marshall on service in Chesterfield in June 1973.
John Jones

With the Bristol RE available on the open market from 1967, East Midland was quick to add the type to its fleet, taking both ECW- and Marshall-bodied examples until 1974. One of seven RELL/ECW buses new in 1968, O518 (PNN 518F) is seen at Matlock waiting to head off to Chesterfield in the summer of 1969. *V. C. Jones*

Coaches during the early NBC period were AECs, Leylands, and Bedfords; C62 (262 PRR), a Plaxton-bodied Leyland Leopard PSU3, was found at Trent's Buxton garage in September 1973.
John Robinson

From 1972 East Midland assumed management responsibility for the Mansfield District Omnibus Co, which company it would absorb fully in 1976. Formed in 1929 as successor to Mansfield District Tramways Ltd, since 1937 Mansfield District had been part of the Midland Counties Electric Supply Co and thus closely associated with Midland General and Notts & Derby; all three were nationalised and so became members of the BTC group in 1948. The first Bristol/ECW-built vehicles were delivered to Mansfield District from 1954; B646 (ANN 566B), a 1964 FLF6G/ECW, is seen on layover in Mansfield *c*1974. This vehicle would be transferred to East Midland in 1976.
Author's collection

Bristol VRL demonstrator HHW 933D was tried in service by Mansfield District in 1967, and from 1970 the standard double-deck type was the Bristol VRT, a trio of VRTSL6Gs with ECW bodies arriving in that year. One of these, B315 (FRB 214H), lays over at Newark behind a Gash single-decker in July 1976.
Charles Dean / Author's collection

With its headquarters at Kingston-upon-Hull, East Yorkshire Motor Services started in 1926 with a fleet of around 30 buses. A member of the BET group the company favoured Leyland and AEC chassis in particular. As far as double-deckers were concerned, AECs were operated in some numbers from the mid-1950s, Bridgemasters, Renowns and Regent Vs featuring in the fleet in early NBC days.

AEC Bridgemaster 703 (4703 AT), like all of its type carrying Park Royal bodywork, heads out of Hull towards Withernsea on a sunny day in July 1972.

A particular operating problem for the company was the 15th-century Beverley Bar, through which much of the fleet was expected to pass. This resulted in the distinctive roof profile on most double-deckers until 1957. Lowering the road beneath helped a little, but still required noticeable alterations to roof-lines until the Bar could be avoided altogether (in 1970), even on low-height buses such as 703. A further distinction with East Yorkshire was that it was one of the few NBC subsidiaries allowed to adopt a blue livery, rather than the regulation red or green. This was later changed, however, and poppy red was subsequently adopted.
Alec Swain / Author's collection

Centre: The last AEC double-deckers were 10 Renowns purchased in 1966, their Park Royal bodies continuing to feature the distinctive 'Beverley Bar' roof profile. No 814 (GAT 814D) looks to be newly painted in NBC poppy red at Bridlington in September 1975.
Charles Dean / Author's collection

Right: East Yorkshire's first rear-engined double-deckers, in 1967, were Daimler Fleetlines, whilst Leyland Atlanteans and Bristol VRTs were also bought in the 1970s. In 1972 a further 20 Fleetlines, dating variously from 1963, 1965 and 1967, were acquired from Tynemouth & District; Alexander-bodied 906 (AFT 789C) of 1965 works a local route in Hull soon after its arrival in the fleet.
Alec Swain / Author's collection

Single-deckers operating in the early NBC period were all on Leyland chassis until a batch of Fords were bought in 1976. Dual-purpose Willowbrook bodywork was fitted to seven Leyland Leopards in 1962; 736 (9736 AT) is seen on arrival from Bradford at London's Victoria Coach Station in 1969. It wears the attractive light blue and primrose coach livery worn before the NBC standard applications came along. *Author's collection*

As the 1960s progressed East Yorkshire also bought batches of the Leyland Panther and Panther Cub. Representing the latter is Marshall-bodied 858 (NRH 858F), seen on layover at Bridlington in September 1975. *Charles Dean / Author's collection*

East Yorkshire also took a pair of Leyland Panthers as coach chassis and, even more extraordinarily, had them fitted with rare Metro-Cammell Athena bodywork. New in 1967, 824 (JRH 324E) arrives in Newcastle in October 1974. *Charles Dean / Author's collection*

The Eastern Counties Omnibus Co was formed in 1930 by the amalgamation of four operators serving Eastern England. At the start of the NBC era it still ran many Bristol Ks, the last surviving until 1971. LKH319 (MAH 319), a 1952 Bristol KSW5G, is seen at work in Norwich on route 92A in August 1971, shortly before withdrawal. This vehicle, in common with a number of others, had had its ultimate destination aperture panelled over. *Author's collection*

In 1973 Eastern Counties released 46 1967/8 Bristol FLFs to be exchanged for Bristol VRs from the Scottish Bus Group. Seen in Cambridge in May 1971, FLF491 (LAH 491E) would end up with Central SMT. *Charles Dean / Author's collection*

In exchange for the 46 FLFs, Eastern Counties received only 30 VRs from the Scottish Bus Group, the remaining 16 vehicles materialising as FLFs from Lincolnshire and Eastern National which were older than those that they had replaced! The VRs came from Scottish Omnibuses (Eastern Scottish), Western SMT and Central SMT; VR333 (NAG 584G), one of eight from Western SMT, is seen in Ely c1975, having arrived from Newmarket. *Author's collection*

An interesting survivor in the 1970s was the second prototype Bristol LS, LL744 (MAH 744), which dated from 1951. Eastern Counties went on to buy the LS in both coach and bus form. Pictured in Norwich bus station in July 1971, a year before withdrawal, LL744 was subsequently preserved by the company. *Author's collection*

Below: There were some notable Bristol LHs in the fleet. Acquired in 1970, LH719 (NHU 100F) was the prototype LH bus and had served as a demonstrator for Bristol Commercial Vehicles; bought from United Counties the same year were five LHS6Ps new to Luton Corporation three months earlier but not used by either company and so re-registered by Eastern Counties. Originally XXE 133H, LHS597 (WNG 103H) is pictured on layover at Ipswich in 1971. *Author's collection*

Left: Eastern Counties bought the Bristol RE for 10 years from 1964. Until 1969 new RELH coaches carried ECW bodywork, the last batch of this combination including RE896 (SVF 896G), seen pausing at Royston *en route* from London to Norwich *c*1974. It carries the white coach livery in which it was repainted in 1972 and displays (just!) its company fleetname, underlined in red, over the front wheel-arch. *Roy Dixon / Author's collection*

From March 1974 Eastern Counties and National Travel (South East) between them took over the Norwich operations of Mascot Coaches. Although the coaching activities subsequently all passed to NT(SE), Eastern Counties retained a pair of Duple-bodied Bedford YRQs, CB993/4 (VVG 538/9K); CB993, seen on layover at Cambridge in July 1974, would last four years in the fleet. *Geoff Mills*

Established as a separate company upon the division of the National Omnibus & Transport Co, the Eastern National Omnibus Co commenced trading in 1930, and a year later Thomas Tilling gained a controlling interest. Following nationalisation in 1948 it standardised on Bristol/ECW vehicles. Over the winter of 1965/6 the company converted 10 KSW5Gs of 1953 to open-top for service at Southend and Clacton. By 1968, however, the former 2387 (WNO 485) had become tree-lopper 0485 seen posing for the camera at Hadleigh depot in December 1969. The last closed-top KSWs were withdrawn in 1971, several achieving fame in the 'On the Buses' feature films. *Geoff Mills*

Southend in April 1976 is the setting for Bristol LD6G 2538 (61 PPU), apparently fresh from the paintshops (although whoever applied the fleetnames clearly wasn't having that good a day!). Eastern National bought its last Lodekkas — including coach-seated FLF6Gs for the London–Southend services — in 1968. *Charles Dean / Author's collection*

Long-established Essex independent Moore Bros of Kelvedon had been acquired by Eastern National in February 1963, and a handful of the 42 vehicles included in the deal survived into NBC ownership. Guy Arab IV/Massey 2018 (581 AOO) was one of two on order at the time of takeover and delivered with various standard THC bodywork features, notably T-type destination screens. Arriving from Chelmsford in full NBC livery, it is seen being pursued through the streets of Colchester by Bristol FLF/ECW 2839 (LWC 665C) in April 1973. *John Aldridge*

In common with its neighbour Eastern Counties, Eastern National was involved in the NBC/SBG Bristol FLF/VR exchanges, receiving 21 VRs in the years 1971/3. Of these, 15 were transferred from Alexander (Midland) in 1971 to become 3005-19 with ENOC, including 3014 (SMS 40H), photographed in April 1976 leaving Southend for Canvey. Registration numbers aside, the Scottish VRs were identifiable by their distinctive destination displays.
Charles Dean / Author's collection

One-time United Bristol LS5G/ECW 2029 (PHN 858) joined the Eastern National fleet as a replacement for similar accident-damaged 1234 (856 ETW). Numbered 1248 by its new owner, it is seen on layover from a Witham working at Braintree under a dusting of snow in December 1969 in the company of Bristol MW5G/ECW 1401(1251 EV). *Geoff Mills*

Clacton-based Bristol MW6G/ECW 1451 (OWC 183D) leaves Colchester for Tiptree in April 1976. This vehicle was originally one of three similar coaches in the Tillings Transport fleet and was new in 1966. Tillings was formerly controlled by Eastern National and subsequently became a constituent of National Travel (South East).
Charles Dean / Author's collection

The Hants & Dorset Motor Services title appeared in 1920 through the renaming of Bournemouth & District Motor Services. The company was owned jointly by Tilling and BAT until the merger and passed to the former in 1942; it thus came under BTC control from 1948, whereafter the Bristol/ECW combination became the standard choice for vehicles. The company's Bristol K variants lasted well into the NBC era, the last KSW6Bs running in service in February 1974. However, lowbridge K6B/ECW 1258 (KEL 701), eking out its last few months of service on schools duties at Eastleigh early in 1969, would be withdrawn that September. *Author's collection*

Hants & Dorset did not take the Bristol VR until 1973, the last full year of the KSW6B, so until then most of its double-deck requirements continued to be satisfied by an army of Bristol Lodekkas. Rare FL6B 1204 (4391 LJ) of 1961 is pictured in April 1976 standing on the upper level of Bournemouth bus station, which sadly would be destroyed by fire that summer. *Charles Dean / Author's collection*

Bristol VRT/ECW 3341 (MEL 562P) is almost new in Portsmouth in April 1976, working from Southampton to Southsea. *Charles Dean / Author's collection*

Over the years a number of vehicles have been modified with a cut-away front to enable the boarding of the Sandbanks Ferry on the Bournemouth–Swanage route. In 1970 all 10 Bedford VAM70/Willowbrook saloons of 1968 were so modified, as demonstrated by 3001 (MRU 64F) coming off the ferry on the Swanage side at Shell Bay in August of that year. *Philip Wallis*

The Hants & Dorset coaching fleet was more interesting than that of many ex-THC companies; not least it included examples of the Bedford VAL — always a popular choice for the enthusiast. Duple-bodied 62 (WEL 802J) was actually an ex-Wilts & Dorset vehicle ('W&D' can still be seen sewn into the headrest covers) and is seen a long way from home in Newcastle. Hants & Dorset also acquired Bedford VALs from Shamrock & Rambler and King Alfred. *Author's collection*

Other Hants & Dorset coaches that were worth more than a passing glance were the various Duple-bodied RESHs and RELHs. Photographed in Southampton in June 1972, 1058 (REL 742H) was an RELH6G, one of a pair delivered in 1969.
Alec Swain / Author's collection

Formed in 1915, Wilts & Dorset Motor Services had, since 1964, been under common management with neighbouring Hants & Dorset and was finally absorbed by the latter on 1 October 1972. The active fleet in 1969 consisted of the usual suspects for an ex-BTC company, the many Bristol/ECW products in stock including KSWs and a couple of rebodied LL6Bs. There were also a number of Bedford buses and coaches bought in the late 1960s together with a few Leylands remaining from the takeover in 1963 of Silver Star Motor Services, Porton Down. The Bristol Lodekka was the most common type of double-decker; 624 (OHR 382), an LD6G/ECW of 1956, is seen passing through the village of Dummer on the very last journey on route 108, the 17.45 Winchester–Basingstoke, on 7 April 1971. *Philip Wallis*

Left: The most modern Wilts & Dorset double-deckers were Bristol FLFs; 204 (470 BMR) leaves Basingstoke bus station on a local service, passing ex-Maidstone & District Leyland Panther/ Willowbrook 688 (JKK 199E) outside the depot, c1972. *Author's collection*

Below left: A number of Bedford VAMs were bought in 1967/8; Willowbrook-bodied VAM70 819 (LMR 739F) poses at Salisbury in 1969. All bus-bodied VAMs were withdrawn by Hants & Dorset in 1974. *Author's collection*

Below: Five Bedford VAM14 coaches were new in 1967, including two-year-old 915 (HAM 501E), seen at Victoria Coach Station in 1969. *Author's collection*

Pictured at Salisbury two ex-Wilts & Dorset Bristol MW6Gs illustrate the transition period; 818 (XMR 948) carries the traditional W&D fleetname on the front and newly applied 'Hants & Dorset' on the side.
Author's collection

Other unusual vehicles in the Wilts & Dorset fleet were 16 Willowbrook-bodied Leyland Panther single-deckers acquired from Maidstone & District in 1971/2 (Hants & Dorset taking a further 17); 696 (JKK 207E) is at Southampton in April 1976. Having been a green fleet in pre-NBC days, Hants & Dorset adopted poppy red in order to retain some hint of the old W&D identity. The Bristol LD alongside still carries the old colours.
Charles Dean / Author's collection

On 30 April 1973 Hants & Dorset took over the well-known and respected Winchester independent R. Chisnell & Sons, trading as King Alfred. This was not a welcome development, as the former was already trading at a loss and could have done without further problems to contend with! The varied fleet of 37 vehicles, all bought new, included AEC Renowns and Bridgemasters, several Bedfords, a number of Leylands, including Atlanteans, and a trio of Metro-Scania single-deckers. AEC Renown/Park Royal 2211 (595 LCG) received NBC livery in May 1974 and is seen soon after on local Winchester route 185.
Philip Wallis

Formed in 1928, the Lincolnshire Road Car Co passed into Tilling Group ownership in 1942, its first Bristol buses arriving in 1944. At the beginning of the NBC era all double-deckers were Lodekkas, the last KSWs having departed in 1968. This was not to last, however, as the first Bristol VRs arrived in May 1969. The last Lodekkas ran in service in the early 1980s, but 2704 (OVL 488), a 1961 FL6G, seen in 1976 on Grantham town service 32, would survive 'only' until June 1978. *Charles Dean / Author's collection*

The standard BTC single-decker of the late 1950s/early 1960s was the Bristol MW, Lincolnshire taking the type regularly from 1958 to 1962, while final batches delivered in 1965 and 1966 brought its total to 62 vehicles. ECW-bodied 2231 (SFU 856) was new in June 1959 and served 20 years with the company. It is seen in Newark in June 1976, having arrived on a 37 journey from Retford. *Charles Dean / Author's collection*

Lincolnshire bought its first Bristol REs in 1964, the initial batch comprising eight RELH6Gs with ECW coach bodies. By the early 1970s four of these had been downgraded for bus work by the removal of their forced-draught ventilation (replaced by opening windows) and the fitting of bus seats. Thus converted in 1971, 1281 (WFE 416) is seen bound for Gainsborough c1975 in full NBC bus livery. *Author's collection*

Lincolnshire had a long association with the Bristol LH, the type being represented in one form or another between 1968 and 1993. Typifying the breed is ECW-bodied LH6L 1036 (JTL 774N), new in July 1975 and seen on layover at Grantham after arrival from Leicester in June 1976. *Charles Dean / Author's collection*

In 1967/8 Lincolnshire bought five Duple-bodied Bedford VAMs. One of the 1968 trio, 1604 (GFE 92F), was photographed on layover at Cheltenham in 1975. *Author's collection*

The first five Bristol VRs entered the fleet in 1969 and included 1904 (JVL 619H), delivered in August. It is seen leaving Lincoln for Skegness on 26 June 1976. *Charles Dean / Author's collection*

One year after the formation of the National Bus Company, on 1 January 1970, a new subsidiary joined the fold. London Country Bus Services Ltd, previously London Transport's Country Bus & Coach Department, began operation with 1,267 buses and coaches running from 28 garages. Its existence was born out of the 1969 Transport (London) Act, which transferred control of London Transport to the Greater London Council. The GLC understandably didn't want responsibility for bus operations in areas many miles from the capital, such areas as Luton, Stevenage, Gravesend and Windsor, so these were formed into a new company. Many of the problems inherited were organisational, the Country Area being dependent on Aldenham Works and subject to a central stores system, creating an urgent need for new overhaul and maintenance procedures, while 70% of the fleet was at least 16 years old. The initial fleet was, of course, pure London Transport, the aforementioned 70% comprising mainly RT and RF types. In May 1971 17-year-old Park Royal-bodied RT4530 (OLD 750) performs on route 801, part of the complex Stevenage town network.
Charles Dean / Author's collection

The oldest single-deckers in the fleet were the RFs (Metro-Cammell-bodied AEC Regal IVs), typified by RF171 (MLL 558), new in 1952, at Aldbury Pond, having completed the short journey from Tring, in July 1974. Tring garage would close in March 1977, route 387 being transferred to Hemel Hempstead.
Lyndon Rowe / Author's collection

The only modern single-deckers to be taken over by London Country were AEC Merlins, all but two dating from 1968. MBS298 (VLW 298G) is pictured working local Hemel Hempstead route 314B in April 1974.
Tony Moyes

Stevenage again, but a bus very different from the RT pictured opposite. The town's network as inherited from London Transport was comprehensive or confusing (depending on one's point of view) and in need of revision. This took place in a number of stages, the third, in July 1971, seeing the introduction of the first 'Superbus' route, for which vehicles carried an attractive yellow and blue livery. Two of the original buses were a new type, Metro-Scania single-deckers; eventually seven of these operated at Stevenage, including MS1 (GPB 19J), pictured at the bus station in April 1973. *Chris Lodington*

The first new double-deckers for London Country were delivered during 1972. These, 11 Northern Counties-bodied Daimler Fleetlines (AF class) diverted from Western Welsh, were closely followed by much greater numbers of Leyland Atlanteans (ANs) bodied by Park Royal or Metro-Cammell. Fleetline AF9 (JPK 109K) shows off its attractive original livery at West Croydon on a Reigate-bound 411 working. The AFs would spend their entire working lives at Godstone garage. *Author's collection*

Also diverted from a Welsh operator were 21 Alexander-bodied AEC Swifts originally intended for South Wales Transport, most entering service in March 1972. Ventilation was notoriously poor, and with non-opening windows much use was made of the roof lights, all open even (as here) on a dull May morning in 1972; only a couple of months old, SMA7 (JPF 107K) arrives in Brighton on a special working, operating from Dartford garage. *Alec Swain / Author's collection*

Left: London Country was a very enthusiastic customer for the Leyland National, taking a total of 543 examples between 1972 and 1979. Some were used on Green Line duties before the introduction of more suitable vehicles, looking smart from the outside but less than impressive to the passenger inside. At least some received coach seating, such as SNC171 (HPF 321N), working between St Albans and London Victoria early in 1976. Such vehicles had replaced 20-year-old RFs in 1974; in 1977 the 713 (and 712) would be withdrawn altogether, replaced by routes 707/717, operated by new AEC Reliance coaches. *Charles Dean / Author's collection*

37

The Maidstone & District Motor Services — a title in use since 1911 — bought its final traditional half-cab double-deckers as early as 1956, in the shape of 22 AEC Regents with Park Royal bodies. These lasted into the NBC era, until 1970/1, along with the remaining 1951 all-Leyland PD2s, the last of which were sold at the beginning of 1970. With only a few months of service left, PD2 5392 (NKT 888) poses for the camera at Hastings in the summer of 1969. *V. C. Jones*

From 1959 Maidstone & District embraced the rear-engined double-decker with enthusiasm, buying firstly Leyland Atlanteans and then Daimler Fleetlines. Still at work in Tonbridge in August 1974, with NBC fleetnames applied to its traditional livery, Atlantean 5492 (492 DKT) was one of the first batch of Metro-Cammell-bodied PDR1/1s delivered in 1959. *Lyndon Rowe / Author's collection*

The Leyland Leopard was chosen for both bus and coach use from 1968. The 1970 intake included 20 PSU4A/4Rs with Marshall bodywork; 3408 (UKE 408H) was barely a month old when photographed at Maidstone in May 1970. In the background is Park Royal-bodied AEC Reliance 3281 (DKT 281). *Lyndon Rowe / Author's collection*

Bristol chassis had been absent from the Maidstone & District fleet for some eight years when the link was restored in the unlikely shape of five 10-year-old MW6G/ECW coaches acquired from United in 1972. No 4702 (7012 HN) basks in the sun outside Gravesend garage in September 1974 alongside 1963 Leyland Atlantean/Weymann 5600 (600 UKM).
Lyndon Rowe / Author's collection

Streamline Coaches of Maidstone sold out to Maidstone & District at the end of 1973, rolling stock consisting of seven Bedford and two AEC Reliance coaches. Within a couple of months all had been repainted into National white, including 4194 (XKO 194J), a 1971 Duple-bodied Bedford YRQ seen on layover at Battersea Coach Park in 1975. The six YRQs were withdrawn and sold to Southern Vectis/ Fountain Coaches early in 1976.
Author's collection

May 1974 saw another takeover, that of John Dengate & Sons, Rye. Eight vehicles were included in the deal — three Fords, four almost-new Leyland Leopards and a Bedford YRQ. One of the Fords was 3244 (SNM 244J), a 1971 Willowbrook-bodied R192, seen in NBC livery on the ramp at Silverhill depot, St Leonards, a little later in 1974. All save the Leopards would be withdrawn in 1977.
Lyndon Rowe / Author's collection

Formed in 1905 as a BET subsidiary, the company known to all and sundry as 'Midland Red' incorporated this in its official title (as the Midland Red Omnibus Co) only in 1974, having previously been titled the Birmingham & Midland Motor Omnibus Co. In BET days it had built the majority of its own buses; the last BMMO-built double-deckers, excepting perhaps the two underfloor-engined prototype D10s of 1961, were the 345 D9s, in production from 1958 until 1966 and withdrawn between 1971 and 1979. Pictured working Banbury local service B3 in April 1973 is 5408 (EHA 408D). *John Aldridge*

Although the D9 was built until 1966, Midland Red had been buying the Daimler Fleetline since 1963 and continued to do so until 1971, after which no new double-deckers would be bought until the company's division into five operating units in 1981, the loss in 1973 of the West Midlands operations, together with 413 vehicles, having reduced the demand for double-deckers. From the 1969 batch is 6218 (UHA 218H), an Alexander-bodied CRG6LXB (Midland Red class D13), seen in Leicester in April 1976. *Charles Dean / Author's collection*

Following the relaxation of legislation to allow 36ft buses, Midland Red introduced its 52-seat S16 class from 1962, although the 8-litre engine rendered the type somewhat underpowered. In the autumn of 1973 a number were hired to City of Oxford, including 5143 (5143 HA), numbered MR36 for its stay and seen at Gloucester Green in September of that year. *John Aldridge*

No fewer than 100 Plaxton Derwent-bodied Ford R192s entered service with Midland Red during 1970/1 and were initially allocated to Banbury, Evesham, Hereford, Ludlow, Rugby, Shrewsbury and Wellington garages. Nos 6348/9 (YHA 348/9J) work city services in Hereford when nearly new. *Author's collection*

The Leyland Leopard was already a familiar type in the Midland Red fleet before it became the NBC standard for coach chassis. One of the 1971 batch of PSU4B/4Rs with Plaxton bodywork (Midland Red class C12), 6453 (AHA 453J) is seen at Leicester on an excursion to Wicksteed Park.
Charles Dean / Author's collection

Above: Although acquired by Midland Red in 1935, Stratford Blue was run as a subsidiary company until finally absorbed under NBC in January 1971. The 49-vehicle fleet taken over was all-Leyland, its only rear-engined double-deckers being a trio of Northern Counties-bodied Atlanteans numbered 9-11, which subsequently became Midland Red 2009-11. Shortly before takeover, 11 (NAC 417F) heads out of Birmingham pursued by a Corporation Daimler and a Midland Red S17 single-decker. Since 1963 Midland Red had bought the rival Daimler Fleetline, and the three Atlanteans, regarded as non-standard, were soon sold to City of Oxford, where they would last until the end of the decade. *Author's collection*

Below: The takeover of Stratford Blue saw the exposed radiator make a return to the Midland Red fleet. The oldest vehicles taken over were a quartet of 1950 Leyland Tiger PS2s rebodied by Northern Counties as double-deckers in 1963. Prior to becoming a Midland Red vehicle, 135 (JUE 351) was photographed heading home at Oxford in August 1970 on a route operated jointly with City of Oxford. The Bristol FLF alongside is United Counties 694 (GBD 694C), working the lengthy (three-hour!) route to Bedford, also a joint operation with City of Oxford. *Philip Wallis*

In 1973/4 Midland Red acquired four operators; Cooper of Oakengates and Green Bus of Rugeley came into the fold in October and November 1973 respectively, whilst Hoggins & Sons of Wrockwardine Wood followed in January 1974. More significant was the acquisition in April of Harper Bros, Heath Hayes, which brought a fleet of 50 buses and coaches together with a number of stage routes, including that from Cannock to Birmingham via Brownhills. An unusual vehicle to receive full National white livery was this Duple-bodied Bedford SB5 2271 (ARE 712J) — formerly Harper 71 — seen on a private-hire working at Shrewsbury in August 1975. *John Jones*

Another unlikely-looking bus to receive Midland Red colours was ex-Harper Leyland PD2A/Metro-Cammell 2228 (HBF 680D), one of a pair bought in 1966. This view was recorded at the Heath Hayes depot in March 1976. *John Jones*

Top left: National Travel (Midlands), effectively a renaming of South Midlands Motor Services, commenced operations in 1974, taking over Worthington Motor Tours, Birmingham, and Don Everall Travel, Wolverhampton; depots were situated in Birmingham and Bilston. Upon takeover the Worthingtons fleet was 100% Ford, all bodied by Duple with the exception of a 12-seater Transit. One of four R192s new in 1967, JOA 271E is pictured in Cardiff in 1975. *Author's collection*

Middle left: Don Everall too had an (almost) all-Ford fleet, perhaps not surprising given that a subsidiary company, Don Everall PSV Sales, was a major Ford dealer. Bodywork was mostly a familiar mix of Duple and Plaxton. Amongst the newest coaches taken over was RUK 525L, a Plaxton-bodied R226 devoid of fleetnames when photographed loading at Leicester in 1976.
Author's collection

Below left: A notable vehicle in the Don Everall fleet was Ford R226/Van Hool NUK 561K, at one time the West Bromwich Albion team coach. *Dave Savage*

Below: Vehicles bought new by National Travel (Midlands) were, with one exception, of Bedford and Ford manufacture. However, a number of Leyland Leopards were acquired from elsewhere within NBC, including six Alexander-bodied PSU3/4RTs that had been new to Hebble in 1968 and came from National Travel (North East) in 1974. With destination box fitted to front dome, EHD 521F heads through Kettering *en route* from Peterborough and Corby to Birmingham in May 1976. *Geoff Mills*

NORTH EAST »
HEBBLE »
SHEFFIELD »

Early in the NBC era Hebble Motor Services was grouped with Yorkshire Woollen and West Riding and from June 1970 assumed the former's coaching responsibilities. Almost a year later, in April 1971, Hebble's stage-carriage work was transferred to Yorkshire Woollen, West Riding and municipal operator Calderdale Joint Omnibus Committee (successor to Halifax JOC); thus Hebble found itself the group's coaching operator. Before all this upheaval, AEC Regent V/ Metro-Cammell 311 (NCP 474) of 1960 heads for Leeds in 1969, pursued by a Huddersfield Corporation Daimler Fleetline. *Author's collection*

Formerly a Hebble vehicle, AEC Reliance/Plaxton HJX 147F pulls away from the stand at Pond Street bus station, Sheffield, in 1975, probably heading for the former SUT garage at Charlotte Road. *Author's collection*

In 1974 Hebble merged with Sheffield United Tours to form National Travel (North East). Having arrived from Hull, former SUT 400 (XWJ 400G), an AEC Reliance/Plaxton — which combination made up the bulk of the fleet — reaches journey's end back on home ground at Sheffield c1975. *Author's collection*

All new coaches taken into stock in 1975 were leased from dealer Kirkby and comprised seven Bedford YRTs — one bodied by Duple with the rest by Willowbrook. New in August of that year, YRT/Willowbrook KWB 471P is seen at Blackpool when new. Just over a year later it was discovered that the registration had been duplicated, so this vehicle subsequently became KWB 477P. *Author's collection*

Formed in 1923, the North Western Road Car Co, operating in Cheshire, Derbyshire and Lancashire, was an early casualty following the formation of the National Bus Company. Around 60% of its stage mileage was lost with the setting-up of the SELNEC Passenger Transport Authority, to which all operations, vehicles and premises within the Manchester area were transferred in March 1972, initially to a subsidiary, SELNEC (Cheshire) Bus Co Ltd. This left mainly rural services in Derbyshire and Cheshire, which were deemed unviable and were therefore split between Crosville and Trent, brought into effect from January and March 1972 respectively. North Western was thus left with just its express services, many based on Manchester, most of which were retained.

Above: A scene at Stockport in June 1969, and centre-stage is Daimler Fleetline/Alexander 254 (JDB 254F) heading out to Cheadle Hulme. New in 1967, the 10 buses of this batch were the last double-deckers to be bought by North Western. The Liverpool-bound coach to the left is Lancashire United 154 (DTF 584B), a Plaxton-bodied Leyland Leopard PSU3/3. *John Aldridge*

Left: In 1957 the company had taken delivery of 42 Leyland Tiger Cubs; of these, 12 were Burlingham-bodied coaches, the remainder being Weymann-bodied buses such as 672 (KDB 672), seen pausing at Hartington before continuing its journey from Buxton to Ashbourne at the end of December 1971. *Tony Moyes*

Buxton in August 1969 and North Western buses a-plenty, in a scene soon to be consigned to history. Nearest the camera is 862 (RDB 862), an eight-year-old AEC Reliance/Willowbrook bound for Manchester 'LMS' (standing for Lower Moseley Street rather than a railway station); behind are a variety of other single-deckers, including Leyland Tiger Cubs and a Bristol RESL6G/Marshall. *John Aldridge*

North Western operated several express services from Manchester to London, all part of the X5 group and each given a suffix letter to identify the route taken. Leyland Leopard PSU3/Alexander 261 (KJA 261F), seen arriving at London Victoria in 1969, has travelled via Birmingham on service X5L, run jointly with Midland Red. North Western built up a sizeable fleet of Alexander Y-types on PSU3 chassis, the combination becoming its standard express coach of the 1960s and early 1970s. *Author's collection*

With the transfer of all stage-carriage work completed by March 1972, North Western was involved solely with express services. One of a pair of short Leyland Leopards with Harrington Grenadier bodywork new in 1964 (and followed by three similar vehicles in 1965), 150 (AJA 150B) is seen heading for Leeds along Great Bridgewater Street, Manchester, in August 1973. *John Robinson*

A little-photographed member of the North Western fleet (and a reminder that non-PSV support was vital to the smooth running of any bus company), Land Rover SDB 767J was one of five purchased in 1970/1. A number were bought over the years and were no doubt useful over the hilly terrain traversed by North Western routes. Pictured at Northwich, it would pass to Crosville in January 1972. *Tony Moyes*

In 1972 North Western's registered office was moved from Stockport to Wilmslow, such that the five Bristol RELH/ECW coaches delivered in that year carried Cheshire (rather than Stockport) registrations. Pictured c1975, 416 (JMA 416L) awaits the homeward-bound hordes at Blackpool. *Author's collection*

The registered office changed again from September 1972, from Wilmslow to Preston, hence the Lancashire registrations on the final North Western coaches — Duple-bodied Leopards delivered in 1973. No 274 (XTF 828L) is seen on layover at Battersea coach park in 1975. *Author's collection*

In February 1974 North Western merged with one-time Ribble subsidiary W. C. Standerwick of Preston and was renamed National Travel (North West). Both constituent fleets were made up largely of Leyland vehicles; ex-North Western 406 (SJA 406K), an Alexander-bodied Leopard new in 1971, is seen parked in Liverpool before working to Newcastle in 1974. *Author's collection*

Above: When Standerwick became part of National Travel (North West) in 1974 it contributed mainly Leylands. Notable exceptions were 30 Bristol VRLLH6Ls with ECW coach bodies, certainly the 'glamour girls' of the fleet. Standerwick, together with Ribble and Scout, had a long tradition of double-deck coaching, the so-called 'White Lady' Leyland PD1s having been introduced as early as 1948. The VRLs seated only 60 (42/18), which allowed for ample luggage space at the rear. The clean, impressive lines are shown off by 57 (LRN 57J), new in 1971, at Battersea in 1975. *Author's collection*

Below: Another notable coach in the fleet, acquired from Ribble in 1976, was the unique Leyland Leopard PSU5/4R with Alexander M-type body similar to those used by the Scottish Bus Group on its Anglo-Scottish services; indeed, this vehicle was used on the London–Stranraer–Belfast service — a joint operation with Western SMT. The impressive bulk of 1200 (RTF 561L) basks in the sun at Battersea coach park during 1976. From 1 April 1977, with the acquisition of National Travel (Midlands), the company was renamed National Travel (West). *Author's collection*

NORTHERN »
GATESHEAD »
SUNDERLAND »
TYNEMOUTH »
TYNESIDE »
VENTURE »

The BET group, unlike the BTC/THC, was keen to retain small subsidiaries. The Northern General Transport Co had the most and began 1969 with five — Wakefield's Motors, Tynemouth & District Transport Co, Sunderland District Omnibus Co, Gateshead & District Omnibus Co and Tyneside Omnibus Co. Wakefield's, which had been under the control of Tynemouth, was almost immediately absorbed into the main fleet, but hitherto independent Venture Transport joined the fold in 1970. Although transfers were common, each company retained its own identity. Inevitably, such a situation would not be tolerated under NBC, and by 1976 all subsidiaries had been absorbed by the main fleet.

In the Northern fleet, perhaps the most affection is reserved for the Routemasters, the only examples of the type to operate from new outside the London area. In need of a trip through the washer, 3113 (FPT 599C) of 1965 leaves Sunderland for Newcastle in January 1975. Just renumbered from 2129, it would remain in service until May 1977, duly becoming the first 'normal' withdrawal, apart from accident victim 3093.
Charles Dean / Author's collection

Unlikely additions to the Northern fleet in the early 1970s were several elderly Bristol LDs from Crosville. Northern also acquired 10 Bristol FLFs from United in 1972 in exchange for Daimler Fleetlines, United being keen to increase one-man operation, but these lasted only until early 1973, when they went to Scotland in exchange for Bristol VRs (which went to United, the Fleetlines returning to Northern!). 2869 (SHN 257F), photographed at Chester-le-Street in April 1973, subsequently passed to Western SMT.
Charles Dean / Author's collection

Leyland Atlantean 1896 (896 EUP), one of nine Metro-Cammell-bodied PDR1/1s delivered to Northern in 1960, loads at Jarrow in June 1972. Creeping in behind is Gateshead & District 124 (BCN 542C), an Alexander-bodied Atlantean of 1965. *Charles Dean / Author's collection*

The NBC era saw the introduction of ECW bodywork into the Northern fleets. No 3229 (NCN 105L), seen in Newcastle in March 1976, was one of a batch of 13 Leyland Atlanteans new in 1972 to Gateshead & District, hence the green livery. *Charles Dean / Author's collection*

Northern was quick to take the new Leyland National, running a number with 'K' registrations. No 61L (NCN 961L) was brand-new when photographed at Jarrow in 1972. *Charles Dean / Author's collection*

By the early 1970s many former BET fleets had been infiltrated by the Bristol/ECW combination. Northern received 24 Bristol RELH6Gs bodied by ECW (14) and Plaxton (10) in 1972, after which it returned to the Leyland Leopard for its coaching requirements. RELH 85L (MCN 885L), on tour in Edinburgh in June 1973, carries the ECW coach body of the 1972-4 period, showing more than a passing resemblance to contemporary Plaxton and Duple designs and looking well in the livery style that preceded National white.
Charles Dean / Author's collection

Tramway operator Gateshead & District began operating buses in 1913 as an experiment, but such was the success of this venture that a new company — Northern General Transport — was formed to run them, commencing operations from the beginning of 1914. Gateshead reverted to tramway operation only, not running any more buses until 5 March 1950, when it replaced its cross-Tyne trams before abandoning them altogether the following year. Most buses bought between 1950 and 1974 were Leylands; this is in fact a Tynemouth vehicle, PD3/4/Metro-Cammell 229 (AFT 929), operating on loan but in full livery and with Gateshead legal lettering. The location is Sunderland Road depot, on 9 April 1972.
Charles Dean / Author's collection

The first single-deckers for Gateshead were six Bristol RELL/ECW saloons in 1971, which ran for only a few months until transferred to Northern General in exchange for a similar number of Willowbrook-bodied Daimler Fleetline saloons. 2822 (LCN 522K) is working local route 52 in July 1972.
Charles Dean / Author's collection

Alone among the Northern subsidiaries, Sunderland District buses were blue, a livery they managed to retain within NBC for a while. The last half-cabs to be bought were 13 Burlingham-bodied Leyland PD3/4s new in 1958. Skulking in the shadows at Worswick Street, Newcastle, is 287 (YPT 287), about to depart on the long route to West Hartlepool in April 1971.
Charles Dean / Author's collection

Much of the Sunderland District fleet was single-deck (69 of a total of 97 in 1974, for example) and was mainly Leyland. Consett-bound 365 (WPT 365F), a Willowbrook-bodied Leyland Leopard PSU3, reverses out of Stanley bus station in September 1973.
Charles Dean / Author's collection

Tynemouth & District first ran buses from 1921, operating a variety of chassis types over the years. The fleet in 1970 stood at 89 vehicles, a mixture of AEC, Daimler and Leyland types, and, in contrast with Sunderland District, these were mainly double-deckers. Two batches of Leyland Titans were in stock when NBC took control in 1969, including 10 PD3/4s with Metro-Cammell bodies that had been new in 1958. Sporting full NBC livery in October 1972 is 229 (AFT 929).
Charles Dean / Author's collection

In an exchange deal with East Yorkshire, in 1972 Tynemouth received six AEC Renowns with Park Royal bodywork. Waiting in St Mary's Place, Newcastle, prior to heading for the seaside at Whitley Bay in July 1973 is 330 (GAT 817D). *Charles Dean / Author's collection*

Five Alexander-bodied single-deck Daimler Fleetlines were delivered to Northern in 1971 only to be hired (and later transferred) to Tynemouth. Seen leaving Sunderland for Hebburn in April 1972 is 328 (KCN 28J). *Charles Dean / Author's collection*

Some 25 Leyland Panthers with innovative Marshall Camair bodywork were delivered to the Northern Group in 1967-9. Three of the 1969 batch went to Tynemouth, including 309 (HCN 45G), seen here in Tyneside PTE-style yellow livery in May 1973. *Charles Dean / Author's collection*

Based at Wallsend, on the south bank of the River Tyne, Tyneside began operating buses in 1930, when the trams into Newcastle were withdrawn. Most buses were Leylands, although the final deliveries in 1973 were Daimler Fleetlines. The two vehicles bought in 1965 were Alexander-bodied Leyland Atlantean PDR1/1s, of which 55 (ENL 355C) looked to be in fine condition when photographed in July 1972. *Charles Dean / Author's collection*

Two Burlingham-bodied Leyland PD3/4s were acquired by Tyneside from Sunderland District in 1971. These had arrived in place of three Bristol RELLs diverted to Northern. Formerly numbered 292 with Sunderland District, 67 (YPT 289) poses beside sister vehicle 295 (YPT 295) at Philadelphia depot in April 1973. *Charles Dean / Author's collection*

The Venture Transport Co had previously been independent and sold out to NBC, operating as a subsidiary of Northern from May 1970 until January 1975. Lightweight, high-capacity vehicles were favoured until the 1960s, when Leyland Leopards became popular. The last Bedfords were six Duple-bodied VAMs of 1967, VC1-6 (SUP 201-6E). On takeover by NBC all except VC1 and VC5 were soon withdrawn, these survivors lasting until 1974. VC1 (SUP 201E) is on private hire in August 1971. *Charles Dean / Author's collection*

Although carrying full NBC dual-purpose livery with Venture fleetnames, Alexander-bodied Leyland Leopard 295 (RPT 295K) was technically a Northern vehicle by the time this photograph was taken in February 1975 at Worswick Street bus station, Newcastle. *Charles Dean / Author's collection*

In line with a policy outlined as early as 1927, The City of Oxford Motor Services, a BET company with tramway origins, had ended the 1960s with a fleet that was almost 100% AEC (even the Dennis Lolines bought in 1961 having AEC engines), although change was in the air with the arrival in 1968 of the first Daimler Fleetlines, AEC having no rear-engined double-deck model to offer. No 334 (334 RJO), a 1963 AEC Renown with Park Royal bodywork, works a local route at Oxford station in October 1975. *Author*

Above left: Following on from AEC Regals and Reliances, Oxford bought the new AEC rear-engine model, the Swift, in 1966/7. Nos 620-7 had Willowbrook bodywork, while 628-38 were bodied by Marshall. Seen at work in the High Street, Oxford, in 1974 is 622 (DFC 622D). *Author's collection*

Above right: Although City of Oxford was notable in that it bought no Leyland Nationals, it did, along with many other NBC subsidiaries, have a flirtation with lightweight chassis in the mid-1970s. One of 25 Willowbrook-bodied Ford R1014s delivered in 1973, 665 (NWL 665M) is seen in Oxford in July 1974 prior to working out to Faringdon, where Oxford also had a depot. *Alec Swain / Author's collection*

Left: Working the 82 from Oxford to Aylesbury is 905 (NAC 416F), a Northern Counties-bodied Leyland Atlantean, one of three acquired from Midland Red (but new to Stratford Blue) in 1971 to speed conversion to one-man-operation. It is March 1972, the location unmistakably Gloucester Green, where a bus station was established in 1935. *Author's collection*

Both previously subsidiaries of the Red & White group, South Midland Motor Services and Newbury & District Motor Services had come under Thames Valley control in 1950, the former bringing with it express licences from London to Oxford and Worcester. The Newbury & District name soon disappeared (although the company was not formally absorbed until 1970), but on 1 January 1971 the South Midland coaching operation was transferred to City of Oxford, the vehicles involved including several Bedfords as well as the more predictable Bristols. One of four Duple-bodied Bedford VAMs new in 1966, 415 (GRX 415D) is seen prior to transfer, in October 1969, engaged on private-hire duties at Didcot station. *Alec Swain / Author's collection*

With the transfer of the South Midland operations from Thames Valley at the beginning of 1971 came a variety of stock, mainly Bristols but including seven Bedfords. Seen at Keswick on its way to the Scottish Highlands on a 12-day tour in September 1975, 37 (YBL 926H) was one of a dozen Bristol LH6Ls, in this case with Duple Northern bodywork. *Charles Dean / Author's collection*

City of Oxford experienced acute vehicle shortages from the late 1960s through to the mid-1970s, due in part to a lack of maintenance staff, as better-paid jobs were available elsewhere, particularly the local car industry. Many vehicles were hired from other operators, both from within NBC and from outside, including Black & White, Red & White, Southdown, Barton and Coventry Corporation. Although this was no doubt a source of fascination to the enthusiast, it was probably confusing for passengers and exasperating for employees! Swindon Corporation also contributed several buses, including Willowbrook-bodied AEC Reliance 140 (AMR 140B), which Oxford numbered SW4; it was on loan from July to November 1973 and is seen outside Wantage garage in the September. Also in view are ex-Aldershot & District AEC Reliance/ Park Royal 69 (425 DHO) and, in the foreground, 640 (PJO 640J), the Alexander-bodied single-deck Daimler Fleetline, unique in the fleet. *John Aldridge*

Oxford also hired a number of Dennis Lolines from Aldershot & District, in 1969/70. Weymann-bodied 493 (493 KOT), numbered A15 by Oxford, was on loan between October 1969 and April 1970, being seen that March in Oxford High Street. Passing on the offside is 391 (MJO 391H), one of the new Daimler Fleetlines with Northern Counties bodywork, 15 of which were delivered over the winter of 1969/70. *Philip Wallis*

An ex-BET company with tramway origins, the Potteries Motor Traction Co, based in Stoke-on-Trent, used its initials as a fleetname — a situation which initially survived the introduction of NBC's corporate image in 1972. At the beginning of 1969 it was operating a sizeable fleet of rear-engined double-deckers. Leyland Atlanteans had been in service since 1959, with the first Daimler Fleetline being introduced three years later. The last half-cabs were withdrawn from passenger service by 1972. One of 15 low-height Leyland Atlanteans delivered in 1961, 867 (867 REH) is seen at work in a rather damp Stoke in June 1976, its uninspiring Weymann bodywork hardly improved by the drab NBC livery. However, with the last of the type remaining in service until 1980, PMT certainly got its money's worth! *Charles Dean / Author's collection*

Wells Motor Services of Biddulph, with origins going back as far as 1914, came under the control of PMT in 1953, running as a subsidiary until 1959. Three Willowbrook-bodied AEC Reliances ordered by City of Oxford were allocated to the Wells fleet in 1955, initially running in green livery. Pictured leaving Hanley for Leek in November 1970, S5626 (WJO 744) was the last to survive, until the end of 1972. *Tony Moyes*

The first year of NBC control saw PMT hire nine 20-year-old Leyland PS2/1s with Weymann bodies from Birmingham Corporation (and its successor, West Midlands PTE). They were hired for varying periods, the last finally being returned in June 1970. 2257 (JOJ 257) no doubt gave an impressive performance climbing up Penkhill New Road, Stoke, in September 1969. *Tony Moyes*

No account of PMT in the early NBC era would be complete without mention of the Daimler Roadliner, 64 of which, mainly buses, entered service between 1967 and 1969. Bodywork on the buses was supplied by either Plaxton or Marshall, the former's being fitted to the final batch, of which 130 (WEH 130G) was photographed at Stafford *en route* to Hanley in August 1969, when but a month old. Poor reliability would lead to the type's early demise, 130 being among the last to go, in 1976. *John Aldridge*

From the mid-1950s until 1971 most of PMT's coaching requirements were met by the AEC Reliance. Added to stock in 1968 were seven Reliances with Alexander 49-seat bodies; 109 (PVT 109F), by now in dual-purpose livery, is seen at Stoke garage in June 1976. On either side are a Bristol RELL/ECW and Ford Transit service van HRE 571N. *Charles Dean / Author's collection*

Following half a dozen Daimler Roadliners PMT turned to Ford for coaches delivered in 1972 (3), 1973 (17) and 1974 (4). One of the final batch to enter the fleet, in June 1974, R1114/Duple 44 (OEH 44M), is seen engaged on private-hire duties at Newark in the summer of 1976 in the company of R226/Plaxton 18 (PVT 118K), one of the trio dating from 1972. Leyland's Leopard subsequently became the preferred choice for coach chassis. *Charles Dean / Author's collection*

Gosport & Fareham Omnibus Co, which traded as Provincial, was another latecomer to the NBC fold, joining in January 1970. The previously independent operator was known as an innovator as far as vehicles were concerned, with many instances of rebodying and rebuilding to its name, perhaps most notably the Guy-Deutz conversions. The fleet in 1970 included numerous Guy Arabs of one form or another, but such non-standard types were soon swept away, initially by draughting in vehicles from elsewhere within NBC and later by new deliveries. Working the company's trunk route between Gosport and Fareham at Brockhurst in August 1970, 55 (EHO 228) was a 1942 utility Guy Arab I with a 1955 Reading body. Withdrawn shortly afterwards, it was subsequently bought for preservation. *Philip Wallis*

Also representing the old order is 24 (CG 9607), one of the two AEC Regals to survive into NBC ownership. New in 1934, it had been rebuilt in 1955 and rebodied by Reading in 1962. Upon withdrawal in 1970 it too passed into preservation. *V. C. Jones*

Following a change of management, Provincial had begun to modernise in 1968/9 with the purchase of 15 Seddon Pennine IV saloons; five second-hand Bristol LS coaches were also bought in 1969. Strachans-bodied Seddon 39 (MHO 190F) of 1968 is seen at Gosport Ferry in March 1972. *Author's collection*

Under NBC influence in 1970, Provincial gained seven AEC Regent Vs from City of Oxford. Seating 65, they had a larger capacity than any previous Provincial bus. Park Royal-bodied 68 (976 CWL) waits at Gosport Ferry on route 1 in March 1972. *Author's collection*

With the AEC Regents came a trio of ECW-bodied Bristol LS saloons, although only two, from Midland General, actually entered service. New in 1955, 35 (XNU 422) works the Gosport–Haslar service in March 1972. *Author's collection*

Below: The first new buses for Provincial under NBC were six Bristol RELL6Gs with ECW bodywork delivered in July 1971, 5 (BCG 105J) being seen at Gosport Ferry prior to working out to Bridgemary in 1972. These had been diverted from Hants & Dorset, under whose wing Provincial now found itself; six Roe-bodied Daimler Fleetlines ordered by Provincial were delivered instead to Hants & Dorset, in 1971. *Author's collection*

Red & White Services had a complex but fascinating history, having been formed in 1930 as an amalgamation of a number of companies operating in Monmouthshire and the Forest of Dean. As a group Red & White also controlled several English bus companies, including Cheltenham District, Newbury & District and South Midland. The group was nationalised in 1950 and the smaller operations were reallocated to existing BTC subsidiaries, of which the main Red & White fleet now became one. The first ECW-bodied Bristols were bought new in 1953; prior to this Albions, Guys and Leylands had entered service in some numbers. By 1969, then, Red and White was exclusively Bristol/ECW, remaining so until 1974. Double-deckers were all Lodekkas of one sort or another; L1060 (10 AAX), a 1960 FL6G, climbs through the centre of Caerphilly in November 1972, passing a cinema showing *Seven Brides for Seven Brothers*. *John Jones*

During 1953/4 some 55 Bristol LS buses and coaches had been delivered, allowing for a good clear-out of older stock. Still active in 1970, U853 (LAX 637) would be amongst the last to be withdrawn, the following year. *Author's collection*

The Bristol MW, successor to the LS, appeared in some numbers from 1957 until 1967, by which time the RE was being delivered. Cardiff in May 1973 is the setting for U2459 (VWO 224), new in 1959, as revealed by the last two digits of the fleet number. Alongside is Bristol RELH6G/ECW RD872 (CWO 291K) working to Neath. *John Aldridge*

Above left: Like the LS and MW, the Bristol RE was bought in both bus and coach form. The first coaches were a dozen RELH6Gs which arrived early in 1966; RC666 (GWO 6D) is seen leaving Liverpool on an Associated Motorways service to Cardiff in 1974. *Author's collection*

Above right: Bristol RE beside the sea; Red & White bought the RE in bus form from 1965 and in 1967 took both RESL and RELL versions, although the latter were to dual-purpose specification. An example of the former, RS1167 (LAX 111E) takes the air at Porthcawl, awaiting its driver before departing for Aberdare in March 1973. *John Jones*

Centre right: Hitherto independent Jones Omnibus Services of Aberbeeg, in the Ebbw Valley, became one of the smallest NBC subsidiaries when it sold out to the state in April 1969. Wearing the blue livery that Jones was permitted to retain, U1561 (889 AAX), a 1961 Leyland Tiger Cub, is seen at Six Bells, Abertillery, while on a PSV Circle tour in April 1975. *John Jones*

The Jones fleet was put under Red & White control, and there were a few transfers between the fleets. Seen at Aberbeeg in August 1973, RC468 (OAX 4F), a 1968 Bristol RELH6L/ECW, was transferred from Red & White in 1972. *John Jones*

Ribble Motor Services was an enthusiastic operator of Leyland PD3s with full-fronted bodywork by Burlingham or Metro-Cammell, the final examples arriving in 1963; it followed these in 1964/5 with 16 Albion Lowlanders with full-fronted Alexander bodywork, its last front-engined double-deckers. One of the 1964 deliveries, 1857 (UCK 857) was photographed at Morecambe in September 1975.
Charles Dean / Author's collection

Ribble bought the Leyland Atlantean from 1959 until 1980. New in 1962, 1811 (RRN 411), a lowbridge Metro-Cammell-bodied PDR1/1 model, is seen at work in Carlisle in February 1975. Ribble had taken over services here from United in January 1969, and by June 1972 all services from the depot had been converted to one-man operation.
Charles Dean / Author's collection

In 1967 Ribble took over Bamber Bridge Motor Services, along with a couple of Weymann-bodied Leyland PDR1/1 Atlanteans. One was a former demonstrator; the other (2295 TE), numbered 1967 by Ribble, had been bought new in 1963 and is seen in the Accrington area *en route* from Clitheroe to Manchester in March 1973. *Charles Dean / Author's collection*

In 1932 Ribble had acquired Blackpool coach operator W. C. Standerwick, which survived as a subsidiary until becoming a constituent of National Travel (North West) in 1974, whereafter the name was gradually dropped. Double-deck coaches were a feature of both Standerwick and Ribble fleets, the last, for Standerwick, being 30 ECW-bodied Bristol VRLLH6Ls delivered 1968/70-2. No 57 (LRN 57J) of 1971 is seen at Victoria when still quite new. *Author's collection*

Much of the single-deck fleet of the 1960s and early 1970s was based on the Leyland Leopard chassis. A Weymann-bodied PSU3/3RT, 816 (ARN 816C) is seen arriving at Newcastle from Carlisle in April 1976. The last of the United vehicles used on this service had been withdrawn a couple of years earlier. *Charles Dean / Author's collection*

Although the Leyland Leopard was for some years the standard choice for single-deckers, Bristol's RE was adopted as soon as it became available and was added to the fleet from 1968 until 1972, when the switch was made to the Leyland National. Displaying the livery used before the NBC standard was adopted, ECW-bodied 336 (NCK 336J) loads for Preston at Wigan in April 1973. *Charles Dean / Author's collection*

National Travel (South East) was formed on 1 January 1974 by the grouping together of London coaching subsidiaries Samuelson's New Transport, A. Timpson & Sons and Tillings Travel (NBC), along with the coaching activities of Eastern National (although the last would have these restored in 1979). Samuelsons operated mainly Leyland Leopards; Duple-bodied KLR 457D was built for sightseeing duties, as indicated by the cove-panel windows. *Author's collection*

Below: The fleet inherited from Timpsons included a Bristol LHS/ECW and a trio of Bedford VALs but comprised mostly AEC Reliances such as 543 EYL, one of a batch of eight Duple Northern-bodied examples delivered in 1963, seen on tour in Dovedale in the summer of 1969. *Author's collection*

Above: On the surface SGF 484L looks to be an ordinary Duple-bodied coach, but deeper investigation reveals it to be a Bristol RELH6L new in 1970 to Isle of Man Road Services, registered 37 UMN. Acquired in 1973 along with another Duple and two Plaxton-bodied RELHs from the same source, it is pictured in National white at Eccleston Place, Victoria, in June 1974. *Geoff Mills*

From March 1974 the Norwich operations of Mascot Coaches were divided between National Travel (South East) and Eastern Counties. All of the ex-Mascot duties passed to NT(SE) in February 1975. During the period of joint operation five Bristol RELH/ECW coaches were hired to Eastern Counties to assist with this work, four carrying 'Mascot National' fleetnames, as demonstrated by 9405 (AVX 966B) at Dover in July 1974. *Geoff Mills*

Among new deliveries to NT(SE) in 1974 was VYM 511M, a Duple-bodied Bedford YRT, seen at Exeter in 1975. *Author's collection*

Used as a promotional vehicle by National Travel (South East) was PFN 879, an ex-East Kent AEC Regent V/ Park Royal acquired in February 1976. It is seen all dressed up for Witham Rotary Club, which hired it to convey carol singers around local estates at Christmas 1976. The location is NT(SE)'s East Anglian base at Kelvedon, the one-time Moore Bros depot taken over by Eastern National in 1963. *Geoff Mills*

The South Wales Transport Co was established in 1914, initially acting as a feeder to Swansea's trams but replacing them completely from 1937. Vehicles of AEC manufacture dominated for many years and, indeed, constituted the entire fleet in 1962, when the absorption of fellow BET subsidiary James of Ammanford brought a number of Leylands. AEC Reliance/Marshall 407 (902 DCY) is seen at work in Swansea in March 1972. *Author's collection*

Above: Neath & Cardiff Luxury Coaches had joined the BET group in 1951, having been formed in the 1930s. Its coaches between Cardiff and Swansea ran via either Neath or the Briton Ferry bridge, their livery prompting the nickname 'Brown Bombers'. Its image was not perpetuated by NBC, and it was absorbed by the South Wales Transport Co on 1 January 1971, by then operating only AEC Reliances; Duple-bodied CTX 985C arrives at Swansea from Cardiff in August 1970. *John Jones*

Below: Also to be absorbed by South Wales in January 1971, Thomas Bros (Port Talbot) was formed in 1951 when BET acquired four independent operators, including Thomas, in the Port Talbot area; a fifth joined the group in 1952. Services included contract and works journeys associated with the local steel industry, and in 1966 Western Welsh transferred certain services to Thomas Bros, thus allowing the closure of its Port Talbot depot. Visible inside Sandfields garage in July 1970 are Leyland Tiger Cubs 117 LNY, 12 CNY and PTX 199, the first two with Park Royal bodywork, the third Weymann. *John Jones*

Third and largest of the operators to be absorbed by South Wales in the early 1970s, United Welsh Services had been formed in 1938 to consolidate a number of Red & White's subsidiary companies in the Swansea area. With the nationalisation of the Red & White empire in 1950, United Welsh was able to buy Bristol chassis for the first time. Bristol MW6G/ECW 13 (277 ECY) pauses at Exeter on its way to Newquay in the summer of 1969. *Author's collection*

A number of Bristol MW6Gs were acquired by South Wales, including examples from Western National in 1970/1. These had previously been Royal Blue coaches and were downgraded for bus work with South Wales. Among the first to arrive, 270 (XUO 719) is seen on layover at Neath in April 1973; it would last until 1974. *John Jones.*

The takeover of United Welsh brought in Bristol Lodekkas to work alongside the standard South Wales double-decker, the AEC Regent V. (Several AEC Renowns and Leyland Atlanteans were acquired in 1972 with the transfer of the Western Welsh depots at Neath and Haverfordwest.) A 1958 Bristol LD6G/ECW, 911 (SWN 154) was formerly United Welsh 318; this June 1975 view was recorded at a Miners' Gala — now sadly a thing of the past — at Edward VII Avenue, Cardiff. *John Jones*

One of two Duple Northern-bodied AEC Reliances new in 1970, 175 (RCY 56H) stands outside Swansea station while on private-hire duty in 1974. *Author's collection*

In February 1974 the well-known coach operator Black & White Motorways was renamed National Travel (South West) and thus formed the core of the new operation. Three other National Travel subsidiaries subsequently joined the fold — Exeter-based Greenslades Tours, Wessex National of Bristol and Shamrock & Rambler Motor Coaches at Bournemouth. Black & White ran coaches throughout the Midlands, South and South West of England, to South Wales and to London and in 1974 was using a mixed bag of Leyland Leopards, AEC Reliances, Bristol RELHs and surviving Daimler Roadliners. In this splendid scene, recorded at Cheltenham coach station in the early 1970s, Plaxton-bodied Leyland Leopard L268 (HDG 368D) waits to head north to Mansfield, while pulling out in front is Duple Northern-bodied Leopard L261 (DDG 261C) bound for Ilfracombe. *John Aldridge*

Greenslades Tours, a company with a history going back to 1912, was an enthusiastic AEC customer, buying little else for many years. The fleet was expanded in May 1971 with the transfer of Grey Cars operations from Devon General, bringing with them more AEC Reliances (as well as some Bedford SBs). Pictured here are Duple Northern-bodied Reliance CFJ 899C and Plaxton-bodied RFJ 825H (fleet numbers not being used until June 1971), new in 1965 and 1970 respectively, wearing the green/white livery style introduced from October 1969. *Author's collection*

The third constituent of National Travel (South West) was Shamrock & Rambler Motor Coaches, independent until 1966 but subsequently closely associated with Hants & Dorset. The fleet, used mainly on tours and excursion work, was latterly predominantly Bedford and included a number of VAL six-wheelers; the trio bought in 1971, all with Duple bodies, included VLJ 232J, seen at Bournemouth carrying its 1975 number (433) — Shamrock & Rambler vehicles being numbered in the 400-49 series within National Travel (South West) 'master scheme' — and the name 'Skua' in tiny letters above. *Author's collection*

Wessex Coaches, Bristol, was another independent to sell out to the National Bus Company, from 1 August 1974. Some 42 vehicles, all Bedfords, were involved, together with all express, tours and excursion licences. The new company was named Wessex National; Wessex Coaches itself continued a limited contract and private-hire operation, for which it retained 38 vehicles. The newest coaches to be acquired by National Travel (South West) were two Bedford YRTs and four YRQs, all Duple-bodied — as were all the inherited vehicles — and all new in 1973. One of the YRTs, 490 (LAE 890L), is pictured with 'Wessex' slipboard over the South West fleetname. *Author's collection*

The first vehicles for National Travel (South West) were 13 Leyland Leopards. Twelve carried 47-seat Duple bodywork, but odd man out, ordered by Greenslades, had a 44-seat Plaxton body more suited for touring. This was 112 (PDG 112M), seen here at Battersea coach park carrying 'Black & White' fleetnames. The intention was that constituent companies' names be retained for private-hire work, excursions etc and 'South West' used for express services, although practice did not always match the theory! *Author's collection*

In 1975/6 many vehicles joined the fleet from elsewhere within NBC, allowing the withdrawal of older stock. Most of these acquisitions were Leyland Leopards, including five Plaxton-bodied PSU4A/4Rs seating only 36. Ex-Ribble 236 (KCK 983H) is seen at Cardiff on arrival from Cheltenham. *Author's collection*

Southdown Motor services had been formed in 1915 by the merger of Worthing Motor Services (whence came the well-loved livery of apple green and cream) and the London & South Coast Haulage Co, together with the 'country' operations of the Brighton, Hove & Preston United Omnibus Co. A BET subsidiary, it was a devoted customer for Leyland products, perhaps its most famous being the 'Queen Mary' Northern Counties-bodied Leyland PD3 which constituted its standard double-decker from 1958 until 1967. A 1964 PD3/4 model, 958 (958 CUF) stands in Brighton's Pool Valley bus station before leaving for Newhaven in April 1976. *Charles Dean / Author's collection*

The traditional Southdown coaching image is represented by Leyland Leopard PSU3/ Duple 1802 (RUF 802H), on tour in Edinburgh in May 1973. *Charles Dean / Author's collection*

Circumstances dictated that Southdown became the biggest operator of Ford coaches within NBC, a situation unimaginable only a few years before. Nevertheless, 37 Duple-bodied R1114s appeared in 1974, to be followed by a further three in 1977. Arriving from Eastbourne, 1432 (SCD 32N) catches the sun at London's Victoria Coach Station in May 1976. *Charles Dean / Author's collection*

At the beginning of 1969 Southdown took over the Brighton, Hove & District Omnibus Co. The latter's oldest rolling stock comprised eight Bristol KS and 49 KSW types spanning the years 1951-7; all would be withdrawn by 1972. All other BH&D double-deckers were Bristol Lodekkas, of various types, delivered up until 1967. A number of these were convertible open-toppers. Seen in closed-top guise at Old Steine in May 1971 is FS6G 2044 (XPM 44), heading west towards Shoreham. Alongside is Bristol FLF6G 2086 (KPM 86E), one of eight FLFs that would pass to Eastern Scottish in 1973 in exchange for Bristol VRs. *Charles Dean / Author's collection*

A number of double-deckers delivered to Southdown from 1969 initially ran in Brighton, Hove & District colours but were repainted green from 1971 as the BH&D identity began to fade away. (Initially a 'Southdown-BH&D' fleetname was applied to vehicles operating from ex-BH&D garages, but the 'BH&D' part was removed in 1974. Ironically an ex-BH&D Lodekka would be the last bus to run in normal service in Southdown green.) Daimler Fleetline/ Northern Counties 2107 (PUF 207H) of 1970 looks a treat in red and cream, also in May 1971. *Charles Dean / Author's collection*

The only saloons to be acquired with Brighton, Hove & District were 10 ECW-bodied Bristol RESL6Gs, delivered just five months before the Southdown takeover. They fitted in well and were not withdrawn until the end of 1982. No 2210 (PPM 210G) basks in the sun at Southsea, with similar 2205 behind. *Charles Dean / Author's collection*

73

'Vectis' (the Romans' name for the Isle of Wight) was the fleetname used by Dodson Bros Ltd and gained its 'Southern' prefix as a result of the Southern Railway's taking a major shareholding in 1929, whereafter the company became the major operator on the Isle of Wight. Railway involvement saw that the company was nationalised in 1948, after which the Bristol/ECW combination became the inevitable choice for buses. Delivered in 1953, the company's last KSWs were followed in 1954 by its first Lodekkas, 21 LD6Gs being required for replacement bus services after rail closures on the island. Seen on layover at Newport, 518/9 (KDL 414/5) would be among the last three of the initial batch to run for Southern Vectis, in September 1975. *P. J. Relf*

Although Southern Vectis had bought its last new K types in 1953 a number were later acquired second-hand, including a quartet of open-toppers from Hants & Dorset in 1964. Seen at work at Sandown, 908 (FLJ 538) would survive until 1974. *Author's collection*

Southern Vectis was quick off the mark in ordering the Bristol VR, the first two arriving in May 1969. A fleet of 73 would ultimately be added to stock, including second-hand examples from the Scottish Bus Group (in exchange for Bristol FLFs) and Hants & Dorset. Seen on layover at Newport is 634 (NDL 634M), new in 1973. Following an accident in February 1974 this bus had been returned to ECW for rebuilding, during the course of which it received a split-level step to aid the elderly in boarding and alighting. *Charles Dean / Author's collection*

Nineteen Bristol REs, in either bus or coach form, were taken into stock between 1967 and 1972. RESL6G/ECW 811 (HDL 26E) from the initial batch is pictured at Ryde with NBC fleetnames on its Tilling-green livery, which it would retain until September 1977.
Charles Dean / Author's collection

Coaching was (and indeed still is) an important part of Southern Vectis operations. The Isle of Wight coaching activities of Shamrock & Rambler (THC) Ltd, set up by the Transport Holding Co in 1967 to take over several local coach operators, were transferred to Southern Vectis in June 1969. One of those takeovers was of Fountain Coaches, whose fleetname and livery of orange and cream were perpetuated. Seen so adorned is Bedford YRQ/Duple 109 (XKO 196J), one of six acquired from Maidstone & District in 1976 but new to Streamline Coaches of Maidstone in 1971.
Charles Dean / Author's collection

Lightweight chassis proved popular on the Isle of Wight, where operations were not too arduous. Southern Vectis famously ran 14 examples of the Bedford VAL, including two from the Shamrock & Rambler fleet. Resplendent in the white livery applied in 1974, 406 (HDL 228E), one of four VAL14s delivered in 1967 with Duple Northern bodywork, basks in the sun at Ryde. Also in the line-up are two VALs from the fleet of Seaview Services and — just visible, in Fountain orange and cream — Southern Vectis 118 (PEL 994G), one of the VALs that came from Shamrock & Rambler. At the far end is Southern Vectis Bristol RELH/ECW 302 (XDL 122L). *Charles Dean / Author's collection*

Established in 1913 and a BET subsidiary, the Trent Motor Traction Co had been an early convert to the rear-engined double-decker, receiving its first Leyland Atlanteans in 1958 and switching to the Daimler Fleetline from 1963. The last half-cabs in the fleet were Leyland PD2s and PD3s, new in 1957 and 1958 respectively. Amid a busy scene in May 1973, Metro-Cammell-bodied PD2/12 767 (KCH 110) prepares to leave Derby for Alfreton. *Charles Dean / Author's collection*

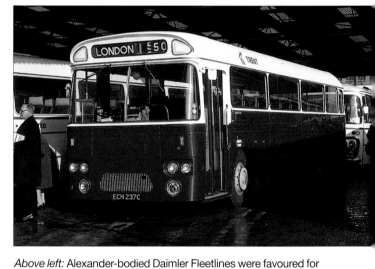

Above left: Alexander-bodied Daimler Fleetlines were favoured for double-deck deliveries between 1965 and 1971, the bodywork order switching to ECW for a final 19 delivered in 1972, after which the Bristol VR/ECW was purchased. Two-year-old Fleetline 541 (DRC 541J), one of the last batch with Alexander bodywork, is seen at Derby on a local working to Mickleover in May 1973. *Charles Dean / Author's collection*

Above: Dual-purpose Willowbrook bodywork was fitted to 20 Leyland Leopards delivered in 1965. Eleven years later and apparently fresh in NBC 'local coach' livery, 237 (ECH 237C) has arrived at London Victoria after a shower of rain in April 1976. *Charles Dean / Author's collection*

Left: In March 1972 the Trent fleet was increased through the takeover of North Western Road Car's operations in the Peak District, along with garages at Buxton and Matlock. The vehicles concerned were either single-deck buses or coaches and were a mixture of AEC Reliances, Bristol RELLs and Leyland Leopards and Tiger Cubs. Willowbrook-bodied Reliance 374 (VBD 931) heads for home from Derby in May 1973. *Charles Dean / Author's collection*

From April 1972 Trent assumed control of the Midland General Omnibus Co, which it would absorb fully by 1977. Although Midland General had been set up in 1920 as a subsidiary of the Notts & Derby Traction Co, by the 1950s it had become the dominant partner. Both were nationalised in 1948 when the Balfour Beatty group sold its bus interests to the BTC; thereafter vehicle policy settled down to the expected diet of Bristol/ECW products, at least as far as buses were concerned. Seen in Nottingham in June 1973, Bristol FLF/ECW 745 (TRB 573F) was from the last batch of new buses delivered to Notts & Derby, passing to Midland General in 1972. Midland General was notable in being one of a select band of NBC operators to wear a blue livery, which subsequently disappeared beneath the poppy red of Trent. *John Jones*

With the Midland General coming under Trent control from 1972, vehicles began to be transferred between the two companies. Early interlopers in the Trent fleet included ex-Midland General Bristol MW6G/ECW 166 (262 HNU), seen loading in Matlock on a local service in July 1975. *Tony Moyes*

Bedford coaches were bought during the late 1960s/early 1970s to work alongside more traditional Bristol/ECW types. The last batch, delivered in 1974, comprised a trio of YRQs with Duple bodies. No 78 (XRC 607M) was almost new when photographed on private-hire duties in Nottingham. *Author's collection*

UNITED ≫

Under Tilling control since 1942, United Automobile Services invested heavily (though not exclusively) in ECW-bodied Bristols including, from 1954 to 1968, variants of the Lodekka. Fresh from the paintshop in October 1974, 398 (5098 HN), an FLF6B of 1962, was photographed working into Newcastle on a service from Blyth worked jointly with Northern General. *Charles Dean / Author's collection*

United was quick to add the Bristol VR to the fleet, the first 20 arriving during 1969. A further 20 of similar vintage were acquired from the Scottish Bus Group in 1973 in exchange for Bristol FLFs. Freshly into service when photographed at Middlesbrough in April 1973, 634 (NGM 172G) had been new to Central SMT. *Charles Dean / Author's collection*

There can be few bus services in the UK where the timetable varies according to the tides, as is the case with that which runs between Berwick and Holy Island (Lindisfarne), off the Northumberland coast. United Bristol MW5G/ECW 2427 (2587 HN) crosses the causeway from the mainland following a light snowfall in February 1974. *D. A. Lawrence*

United built up an impressive fleet of Bristol REs in both bus and coach form, the first arriving in 1962 and the remainder following over a 10-year period from 1964. A 1972 RELH6G with Plaxton coachwork, 1294 (NHN 794K) was caught in traffic while on tour duty in Dumfries in September 1975.
Charles Dean / Author's collection

In February 1967 United took over independent Wilkinson's of Sedgefield, in a deal that included 17 vehicles, three of which were still on order. The only Bedford was FPT 873C, a 1965 Plaxton-bodied SB5, which became United 1073 and was subsequently painted in United's coach livery of olive green and cream, which had its origins in the Orange Bros firm acquired in 1934. Seen in September 1971, 1073 would be withdrawn in 1974.
Charles Dean / Author's collection

Two further County Durham independents taken over by United were Gillett Bros of Quarrington Hill (in October 1974) and Shaw Bros of Byers Green (in January 1975). From Gillett came 23 vehicles — mainly AEC Reliances — and routes from Hartlepool to Durham and Bishop Auckland. Seen in Hartlepool bus station in October 1975, 4003 (6301 UP), a Plaxton-bodied AEC Reliance new in 1963, has arrived on a working from Bishop Auckland.
Charles Dean / Author's collection

The company formed in 1913 as the Wellingborough Motor Omnibus Co changed its name in 1921 to the 'United Counties Omnibus & Road Transport Co', becoming the United Counties Omnibus Co in 1933. It had been controlled by Tilling since 1931, and at the start of 1969 it still had in stock a large number of Bristol Ks — mainly KSWs. Seen at Stotfold Green in 1970 on a 97 journey from Hitchin, 895 (CNH 715) would be withdrawn that October. United Counties' last KSW was retired from passenger service in 1973. *Author's collection*

One of the earliest takeovers of the NBC era was that of well-known and long-established operator Birch Bros, which sold its rural routes in Bedfordshire and Northamptonshire to United Counties in September 1969. Twelve vehicles were involved — all Leyland Leopards, bodied variously by Willowbrook, Park Royal and Marshall and built to either coach or dual-purpose specification — together with a garage at Rushden. One of four Marshall-bodied Leyland PSU3/4Rs, 234 (DUC 73C) paddles through Sutton Ford on a private-hire working in May 1976. *Chris Lodington*

Luton Corporation Transport was taken over by NBC at the beginning of 1970, operations passing to United Counties, with which it had a working agreement. Luton's 82-vehicle fleet comprised a motley collection of half-cab double-deckers and 30 nearly new Bristol RELLs (with 10 more on order). The former lasted with United Counties only until 1974, while the RELLs fitted in rather better, some surviving until the early 1980s. There were also five Bristol LHS6Ps, but these were used neither by Luton nor United Counties before passing to Eastern Counties. Formerly Luton 154, United Counties 814 (WTM 154), a 1959 Leyland PD2/30 with Weymann bodywork, waits in Bridge Street in May 1972 (not long before withdrawal) to work a 43 out to Whipsnade — not an ex-Corporation route and quite rural beyond Dunstable. *Chris Lodington*

Two generations of United Counties Bristol/ECW double-decker at Bedford bus station in June 1973. VR 761 (VNV 761H) takes on a good load for Biggleswade while FLF 731 (LRP 731E) waits to leave for Luton, although neither bus can manage to display a destination blind. Nowadays buses load 'nose in' at Bedford, and the whole area has been earmarked for redevelopment. *John Aldridge*

Along with many other NBC subsidiaries, United Counties was obliged to take lightweight chassis during times of vehicle shortage in the 1970s, and large numbers of Bedford YRT and YRQ types, together with a few Ford R1014s, entered the fleet during the period 1973-6. Seen at Royston when still quite new, YRT/Willowbrook 105 (RBD 105M) was part of the 1974 intake. It is on layover from route 188, a Wednesdays- and Saturdays-only facility serving villages in the Biggleswade and Royston areas. The blue fleet-number plate with black edges reveals 105 to be a Biggleswade vehicle. Standing alongside is a Ford of local independent operator Richmond of Barley. *Roy Dixon / Author's collection*

In 1968 work began on construction of the new city of Milton Keynes, encompassing Bletchley, Wolverton, Stony Stratford and the surrounding villages. United Counties operated most of the bus services. Minibuses first joined the fleet in 1975, when a dial-a-bus service was introduced in association with the Milton Keynes Development Corporation. From 10 March six Deansgate-bodied Mercedes-Benz L406Ds, fitted with 15 coach seats and painted in a yellow livery with the control centre's telephone number prominently displayed, ran in the Woughton area. Seen on the service when new is 2 (HBD 168N). Subsequently further small-capacity buses would be added to the fleet, usually for specific schemes. *Author's collection*

WEST RIDING »
YORKSHIRE »

Formed in 1922, the West Riding Automobile Co was originally a subsidiary of a tram operator, the Wakefield & District Light Railway Co, although the trams were abandoned in 1932. Negotiations to sell to the British Transport Commission in 1948 came to naught, and the company remained independent until sold to the Transport Holding Co in October 1967. Duly passing to the National Bus Company in 1969, it was combined with two ex-BET companies — Hebble and Yorkshire Woollen — as the 'West Riding Group'. In vehicle terms West Riding was perhaps best known for its loyalty to the Guy Wulfrunian, a low-height, front-engined, front-entrance double-decker, of which 137 were built between 1959 and 1965, all but five ending up with West Riding, including a few second-hand examples. However, the type was problematic in service, particularly with regard to the independent front suspension and disc brakes (not to mention the uncomfortable driving conditions), and all would be gone by 1972. Roe-bodied 1025 (BHL 376C), one of the last to be built, in 1965, is seen leaving Wakefield for Bradford in 1969. *Chris Lodington*

West Riding also ran large numbers of more conventional Roe-bodied Guy Arab IVs delivered in the mid-1950s, four of which — 457/9/33/44 (KHL 854/6/30/41) — are seen withdrawn at Dewsbury in 1976. They represented the last green-and-cream buses in the fleet and had been the last lowbridge buses in NBC passenger service. *Charles Dean / Author's collection*

The mass withdrawal of the unsatisfactory Guy Wulfrunians led to the acquisition of replacements from elsewhere within NBC. Bristol Lodekkas, in particular, were drafted in during 1969/70, including 28 from Bristol Omnibus, many of which dated from only 1965/6. FLF6G/ECW 543 (HHY 182D) of 1966 is seen in Leeds in March 1975. *Charles Dean / Author's collection*

In 1970 West Riding inherited all five Northern Counties-bodied Dennis Lolines new to the Halifax Joint Omnibus Committee. Heading out of Wakefield in August of that year is 467 (FCP 303E). *Roger Holmes*

In 1966, unable to buy more Guy Wulfrunians, West Riding had turned to the Leyland Atlantean, buying 25 Roe-bodied examples. From 1968 until 1972 all new double-deckers were Daimler Fleetlines; thereafter the Bristol VRT became the standard. Northern Counties-bodied 721 (BHL 621K) was one of the final batch of Fleetlines and was photographed in Leeds when three years old, in March 1975. *Charles Dean / Author's collection*

In the 1960s West Riding favoured Bedford chassis for its coaches and dual-purpose vehicles, buying VALs, VAMs and SBs. As the 1970s progressed the Leyland Leopard became standard, although Alexander was perhaps a less obvious choice of bodywork for the 1975/6 intake, of which 378 (HWY 718N) was photographed in Leeds in March 1975. *Charles Dean / Author's collection*

As its name implied, the Dewsbury-based Yorkshire Woollen District Transport Co served the mill towns of southwest Yorkshire. In common with West Riding, its early days were concerned with tramways. Buses were running in 1913, only to cease in 1921 and resume in 1924. Hitherto a BET subsidiary, Yorkshire Woollen experienced changes under NBC, with the transfer in 1970 of all coach operations to Hebble and the merging of management and administration with West Riding at Wakefield in 1971. Vehicle-wise, Leylands had been the traditional choice over the years, yet in early NBC days the fleet produced quite a variety of rolling stock. Interesting survivors included six Leyland PS2 single-deckers dating from 1950, rebodied as double-deckers by Roe in 1963; 502 (HD 8551) is seen in Dewsbury c1973. *Author's collection*

In 1969/70 the company experienced severe vehicle shortages, which resulted in a final fling for a number of elderly vehicles, including Bristol KSW6Bs from United and rebuilt K5Gs from West Yorkshire. One of the former, 165 (SHN 713) is seen at work in Dewsbury in January 1970. *Tony Moyes*

A variety of double-deck types entered the fleet during the 1960s, including both Daimler Fleetlines and Leyland Atlanteans. Representing the latter type is Alexander-bodied 588 (DHD 220E) of 1967, seen at Dewsbury in the summer of 1973. *Charles Dean / Author's collection*

In 1975/6 Yorkshire Woollen took delivery of 11 Roe-bodied Leyland Atlanteans, among them 767 (MUA 864P), seen when new in Leeds. *Author's collection*

Four Harrington-bodied AEC Reliances of 1955 vintage were acquired from Maidstone & District in 1968 and worked for a further two years or so. Seen in Dewsbury in 1969, apparently on stage service, is 437 (TKM 347). *Michael Fowler*

Yorkshire Woollen was a coach operator for only a short period within NBC, as from April 1970 all coaching activities, including the depot at Liversedge, were transferred to Hebble. The vehicles involved were mainly Leyland Leopards but included 14 10-year old AEC Reliances. Seen on home ground in Dewsbury, 411 (EHD 526F), an Alexander-bodied Leopard dating from 1968, heads for Coventry a few months before transfer, in 1969. *Author's collection*

Dating from 1928, the West Yorkshire Road Car Co was latterly a THC company and was thus very much Bristol/ECW-biased. A fleet list for April 1970 included only four exceptions — Bedford VAM14 buses bought in 1967 — and even these carried ECW bodywork. Typical therefore was this Bristol FS6B, 1772 (839 DYG), seen on a Keighley local service in March 1976. *Charles Dean / Author's collection*

Buried within the aforementioned 1970 fleet list were one or two unusual entries, such as the four Bristol LS/ECW coaches which had come from Eastern National (although new to Tillings) in 1966. CUG43 (PYO 758) had been new in 1955 yet was still on front-line duties — on an express working to Birmingham — when photographed *c*1970 under the trolleybus wires in Bradford. West Yorkshire had adopted a prefix system to its fleet numbering (CUG signifying **C**oach, **U**nderfloor **G**ardner engine), but in October 1971 this was abandoned in favour of an all-numerical system; CUG43 was allocated 1083 but was withdrawn at around this time and so may not have actually carried this. *Author's collection*

Below: Another photograph taken before the 1971 renumbering illustrates two generations of smaller-capacity Bristol/ECW buses. Seen outside Grassington garage are LH2 (YWT 700G), a 1969 LH6L, and KSMA2 (808 BWR), an SUL4A. West Yorkshire had 17 SUL4As (and one SUL4P), being one of the few operators to take this model. *Author's collection*

Minibuses and minicoaches did not feature much in the early years of NBC, and those that did tended to be used on special services. West Yorkshire leased a pair of Ford Transit/Deansgate 'Chauffeur Coaches', including 1116 (TWW 221L), for a dial-a-ride service in Harrogate, which began in October 1972. *Author's collection*

Two generations of West Yorkshire single-decker at Bradford in July 1973. Both vehicles appear to be in excellent condition; 1069 (8126 WX) is a Bristol MW6G/ECW downgraded from coach to dual-purpose status, while 1380 (UWR 123L) is a recently delivered RELL6G/ECW bus.
Charles Dean / Author's collection

Left: When West Yorkshire bought out well-known independent operator Samuel Ledgard in October 1967, almost all of the latter's fleet of over 100 vehicles found no use with the new company. Exceptions were a couple of Daimler CVG6s, six AEC Regent Vs and this coach, numbered CF1 (8848 WY). A Duple-bodied Ford 570E, it had been new in 1961 to Waterhouse, Crawshawbooth, passing to Ledgard in 1963; seen on a private-hire job at Skipton, it would survive with West Yorkshire until September 1969, thereby enjoying nine months in NBC ownership.
Author's collection

Right: An unusual feature of West Yorkshire was the operation jointly with the local authorities of the fleets in Keighley and York. Keighley-West Yorkshire Services had been set up in 1932 and lasted until the end of 1973. Displaying Keighley-West Yorkshire fleetnames is Bristol RELL6G/ECW 2238 (LWR 883K), seen in April 1973 in Preston — a fair way from its usual haunts, one would imagine. The prospect of a journey across the Pennines to Leeds in a bus-seated RELL doesn't exactly fill one with enthusiasm — a masochists' outing, perhaps?
John Jones

West Yorkshire provided buses in York under the terms of a joint arrangement with the city council, in force since 1932. Vehicles were drawn from the main fleet, among them 3749 (147 CWR), a Bristol FS6B/ECW, seen at work in the city c1975.
Author's collection

In November 1969 the Western National Omnibus Co took over the Southern National Omnibus Co, the two fleets having grown increasingly close in THC days. At this time the double-deck fleet was composed mainly of Bristol Lodekkas; although there was still a sizeable contingent of Bristol KS and KSW types, their demise was swift, all having disappeared from passenger service by 1971. FLF6B/ECW 2038 (418 PTA) of 1964 leaves Plymouth Bretonside bus station to begin the 74min journey to Kingsbridge in April 1976. *Charles Dean / Author's collection*

A dozen 41-seat Bedford VAM5/ECW — an unusual combination — were bought in 1967 as a stopgap between the last Bristol SUL4As and the first Bristol LH6Ls, delivered in 1966 and 1968 respectively. Pictured in the Cornish village of Porthscatho on its way to St Mawes in September 1969 is 710 (KDV 140F). *Lyndon Rowe / Author's collection*

Although the Bristol VR was added to the fleet from 1969, interesting non-standard types included five Leyland Atlanteans acquired from Western Welsh in April 1972, when less than a year old; 1023 (VUH 380J) is seen in Plymouth on layover between journeys on the lengthy route to Looe, in Cornwall. *Charles Dean / Author's collection*

As might be expected, the little Bristol LH found favour for rural work in the West Country, and Western National took the type in some quantity. Ordered by Southern National and delivered as part of the 1970 intake, 1570 (TTA 737H) is seen in August 1974 at Woolacombe while on layover prior to returning to Ilfracombe on route 303.
Roy Dixon / Author's collection

Western National and (in pre-NBC days) Southern National provided Royal Blue coaches for use on express work. The Bristol RELH featured from 1964 and was bought until 1975, although later examples carried Plaxton rather than ECW coachwork. ECW-bodied 2378 (LDV 850F), new in 1968 to Southern National, is seen at Oxford in February 1973 while working an Associated Motorways service to Portsmouth, possibly from Northampton.
John Jones

In 1973 the Royal Blue fleet received 10 Bristol LH6Ls with 7ft 6in-wide Marshall bodies, intended for the narrow roads around Dartmoor and Exmoor, where tour work was undertaken. These were the last vehicles to be delivered in blue and white; by 1976, when 1321 (NTT 321M) was photographed at London Victoria, National white was the order of the day.
Charles Dean / Author's collection

The Exeter-based Devon General Omnibus & Touring Co had been a BET subsidiary and during the 1960s had bought both Leyland Atlantean and AEC Regent V chassis to satisfy its double-deck requirements. A bird's-eye view at Plymouth in 1969 sees 501 (501 RUO), a 1964 AEC Regent V/Willowbrook, on layover after a journey on either route 128 (from Torquay) or the 129 (from Exeter), both joint operations with Western National. Behind is a fine array of 1960s coaches. *Colin Martin*

Municipal bus operation in Exeter passed to Devon General on 1 April 1970, ending a co-ordination agreement in force since 1947. On takeover, Devon General vehicles in Exeter were temporarily housed at the Corporation depot, pending construction of a new garage in the city. The Exeter fleet consisted mainly of Leyland and Guy double-deckers, although the latest deliveries had been short Leyland Leopards and Leyland Panthers. Five Massey-bodied Leyland PD2As had been delivered each year from 1961 to 1965; 299 (DFJ 899C) of the 1965 intake is seen at work in the city on route D in April 1976. *Charles Dean / Author's collection*

In January 1971 Devon General was itself taken over by ex-THC Western National, although its buses retained red livery, complete with Devon General fleetnames. The first Bristols to work for Devon General appeared in 1971 in the shape of ECW-bodied VRs. One of a batch of nine, 546 (VOD 546K) is seen in Exeter in April 1976. *Charles Dean / Author's collection*

In 1972 Western National took delivery of 12 Marshall-bodied Bristol LHS6Ls, of which six were allocated to the Devon General fleet. Illustrated is 91 (VOD 91K), probably when new, working to Sandford on a route formerly operated jointly with Exeter Corporation.
Author's collection

Devon General's Grey Cars coaching operations passed to Greenslades Tours in May 1971. Duple Northern-bodied AEC Reliance 39 (HOD 39E) boards the ferry at Dartmouth to cross the River Dart to Kingswear while on tour duty in July 1969.
Colin Martin

Western/Southern National types also appeared in Devon General livery. In 1975 seven Bristol MW6G/ECW coaches of 1966 were modified for bus work (albeit retaining their coach seats), being repainted in NBC red/white 'local coach' style and renumbered accordingly. New as Southern National 1417, 2978 (EDV 547D) sweeps out of Exeter bus station bound for Kenn — a journey of around half an hour — in April 1976.
Charles Dean / Author's collection

Established in 1927 as South Wales Commercial Motors the Western Welsh Omnibus Co adopted this title in 1929 when the GWR acquired a shareholding. A BET subsidiary from 1931, it had a preference for Leyland vehicles and became an early devotee of the Atlantean, which type first appeared in the fleet in 1960. Delivered in 1962, LR3062 (361 ABO), a Weymann-bodied PDR1/1 model, waits at Cardiff in April 1976.
Charles Dean / Author's collection

Perhaps surprisingly, following early experience with Atlanteans Western Welsh reverted front-engined types for double-deckers. One of 21 Weymann-bodied Leyland Titan PD2A/27s delivered in 1963, H1463 (903 DBO) was caught heading up the A470 at Cilfynydd, near Pontypridd, on its way home from Barry Island with a private-hire party. Under NBC control Western Welsh was managed jointly with Red & White, and by the time this photograph was taken, in July 1975, a common fleet-numbering scheme had been adopted.
John Jones

Western Welsh also took the AEC Renown, which model replaced the Bridgemaster and used Regent V components in a low-height form. Bodied by Northern Counties, L6365 (BKG 719C) is seen on a local route in Newport in April 1976.
Charles Dean / Author's collection

The Leyland Leopard was favoured for both bus and coach work. A Willowbrook-bodied PSU4/2R new in 1971, 1509 (TKG 509J) arrives at Carmarthen from Cardiff in October 1973, passing a rather battered little Austin A35 outside a local garage. *John Jones*

The first Leyland Nationals entered the fleet in 1974/5, including N474 (GHB 790N), seen on layover in Cardiff in April 1976. *Charles Dean / Author's collection*

Based at Porth in the heart of the South Wales coalfield, the Rhondda Transport Co had only a short period within NBC before being absorbed by fellow ex-BET company Western Welsh in January 1971. Pictured in Cardiff when new in 1969 is Northern Counties-bodied Leyland Atlantean 502 (VTG 502G). *V. C. Jones.*

As a result of pressure from the public, the Rhonnda fleetname was retained on buses running from Porth, disappearing only in 1978, upon the formation of National Welsh. AEC Regent V/ Northern Counties H8065 (ETX 487C) is seen in Pontypridd in April 1976. *Charles Dean / Author's collection*

Set up by BET in 1902 as the Barnsley & District Electric Traction Co, the Barnsley-based Yorkshire Traction Co was an avowed Leyland supporter. Its final half-cab buses bought new were 10 PD3A/1s with Roe bodywork, dating from 1965; 737 (CHE 308C) heads for Barnsley in September 1975, two years before the entire batch was withdrawn and sold.
Charles Dean / Author's collection

Yorkshire Traction bought the Leyland Leopard from 1962, for both bus and coach use; 530 (CHE 530K), one of a dozen 45-seat Marshall-bodied PSU4 buses new in 1972, loads at Barnsley in April of that year. From 1973 the company would turn to the Leyland National for its single-deck requirements.
Roger Holmes

Three Plaxton-bodied Leyland PSU3/3RT Leopards made up the total coach intake for 1965. By March 1975 all were in National white; 4 (CHE 303C) arrives in Sheffield at the end of a five-hour journey from Blackpool in March 1975.
Charles Dean / Author's collection

Above: County Motors (Lepton) Ltd, Huddersfield, was taken over by Yorkshire Traction on the first day of 1969, having previously been owned jointly by Yorkshire Traction, Yorkshire Woollen — both formerly BET companies — and independent West Riding. The fleet inherited by NBC included an interesting quartet of Guy Arab IVs with lowbridge Roe bodywork, dating from 1958. Looking in fine fettle in Doncaster in September 1969 is 685 (NCX 176). Three of the four, including 685, survived to give Yorkshire Traction a couple of years' service before being sold for scrap, although the fourth had been withdrawn during 1969. *Roger Holmes*

County also contributed a number of Leyland Leopards, such as Marshall-bodied 393 (BCX 213B), seen at Huddersfield in March 1976. *Charles Dean / Author's collection*

Also coming under Yorkshire Traction control from 1 January 1969, the Mexborough & Swinton Traction Co was another ex-BET company, notable for its operation of trolleybuses until 1961. The fleet as at takeover was mainly Leyland but included Daimler Fleetlines and Bedford coaches. A lowbridge Weymann-bodied Leyland Atlantean new in 1962, 692 (8413 YG) is seen in September 1975 loading in Doncaster for Rawmarsh, where Mexborough & Swinton had its depot and headquarters. *Charles Dean / Author's collection*

Under the ornate ironwork of Durham bus station, United 291 (8111 HN),
a Bristol FLF/ECW, departs for Sunderland on a damp August day in 1974.
Charles Dean / Author's collection

Bibliography

The following publications have been useful in the compilation
of this volume:

The Bristol KSW by Graham Jones and Allan Macfarlane
(OPC, 1985);

The Bristol LH by Geoff Mills (OPC, 1984);

The Bristol Lodekka by David G. Savage (OPC, 1985);

The British Bus Story: Early 'Seventies by Alan Townsin (TPC, 1987);

Lincolnshire Road Car 75 by Graham Wise (NBC Books, 2003);

London Country in the 1970s by Steve Fennell
(Ian Allan Publishing, 2003);

A National Bus Company Album by Ray Stenning (Viewfinder, 1979);

North Western, Volume II by Eric Ogden (TPC, 1981);

*A Pictorial Tribute to the Bristol Omnibus Company and Associated Fleets,
1936-1983* by Allan Macfarlane (OPC, 1985);

A Pictorial Tribute to the National Bus Company, 1981
by D. R. & A. J. Kennedy (OPC, 1982);

Provincial — The Gosport & Fareham Story by Patrick Miller
(TPC, 1981);

The Years before National — 1948-1968 by Ray Stenning
(Fleetline Books, 1982);

Various 'Fleetbooks' published during the 1970s by A. M. Witton;

Various 'Fleet Histories' published by the PSV Circle;

Various editions of *Buses* and *Buses Extra* magazines
(Ian Allan Publishing);

Various editions of *Classic Bus* magazine
(Classic Bus Publishing);

Various timetables and other NBC publicity material.